SARA L. WESTON

The Ancient Huntress

Contents

Preface

"The Ancient Huntress" is an invitation to question, to explore, and to appreciate the rich diversity of human experience across time. It is a call to challenge preconceptions and embrace a more inclusive and accurate portrayal of our ancestors. As we embark on this intellectual expedition, may we glean insights that not only reshape our understanding of the past but also illuminate the path forward, fostering a greater appreciation for the resilience, intelligence, and agency of the ancient huntresses who walked before us.

Acknowledgement

To the readers who embark on this intellectual journey with me, I extend my deepest appreciation. Your curiosity and engagement with the narratives presented in this book contribute to the ongoing dialogue about our shared human history.

I acknowledge the multitude of voices and perspectives that have engaged in explorations and published research, all of whom have helped shape the information written in "The Ancient Huntress," I recognize that the quest for knowledge is a collective endeavor. May this work inspire continued exploration, challenge assumptions, and foster a deeper appreciation for the diverse and dynamic roles played by women in the tapestry of our prehistoric past.

1

Chapter 1

Introduction

"The Ancient Huntress" delves into this captivating exploration of prehistoric societies, with a keen focus on the often overlooked role of women in these ancient civilizations. This book seeks to unravel the intricacies of gender dynamics by shedding light on the lives of the ancient huntresses—women who defied conventional norms and played active, pivotal roles in their communities.

As we embark on this journey through time, the chapters within "The Ancient Huntress" will guide readers through the evolving understanding of prehistoric gender roles. By scrutinizing assumptions that have lingered for centuries, we aim to present a more nuanced and accurate portrayal of the diverse responsibilities shouldered by both men and women in early human societies.

1.1 Understanding Prehistoric Gender Roles

The conventional portrayal of prehistoric gender roles has long depicted men as hunters and women as gatherers, perpetuating the notion that women played a passive role in early human societies. However, recent research and archaeological findings have challenged this narrative, revealing a more complex and nuanced understanding of prehistoric gender roles. This chapter aims to explore the evolving understanding of prehistoric gender roles, highlighting the significance of challenging assumptions and the methodologies used in this research.

1.1.1 The Evolution of Gender Roles

To understand prehistoric gender roles, it is essential to examine the evolution of these roles over time. Early human societies were characterized by a hunter-gatherer lifestyle, where both men and women played crucial roles in ensuring the survival of their communities. While men were traditionally associated with hunting, recent evidence suggests that women also actively participated in hunting activities. This challenges the notion that gender roles were fixed and rigid, highlighting the fluidity and adaptability of early human societies.

1.1.2 The Significance of Challenging Assumptions

Challenging long-held assumptions about prehistoric gender roles is of paramount importance. By questioning these assumptions, researchers can uncover new perspectives and shed light on the lives of our ancient ancestors. This shift in perspective not only challenges traditional narratives but also promotes a more inclusive understanding of prehistoric societies. It allows us to recognize the agency and contributions of women in early human communities, breaking free from the constraints of gender stereotypes.

1.1.3 Research Methodology and Sources

To explore prehistoric gender roles, researchers employ a variety of methodologies and sources. Archaeological evidence, such as artifacts, cave paintings, and burial sites, provides valuable insights into the activities and roles of ancient societies. Paleontological discoveries, including fossil remains and isotopic analysis, offer further clues about the diet and physical activities of early humans. Anthropological studies, examining contemporary hunter-gatherer societies, provide comparative insights into the potential roles of women in prehistoric communities.

Researchers also rely on interdisciplinary approaches, combining the expertise of archaeologists, anthropologists, paleontologists, and other specialists. This collaborative effort allows for a more comprehensive understanding of prehistoric gender roles, drawing on diverse perspectives and methodologies. By integrating various sources and research techniques, scholars can reconstruct the lives of ancient huntresses and challenge the prevailing narratives surrounding prehistoric gender roles.

In conclusion, the understanding of prehistoric gender roles is undergoing a transformative shift. Recent research and archaeological findings have challenged the conventional portrayal of men as hunters and women as gatherers. This evolving understanding highlights the importance of challenging assumptions, recognizing the agency of women in early human societies, and promoting a more inclusive understanding of prehistoric gender roles. By employing diverse research methodologies and interdisciplinary approaches, researchers are uncovering the rich and complex lives of our ancient ancestors, shedding light on the egalitarian nature of early human societies.

1.2 The Evolution of Gender Roles

The conventional portrayal of prehistoric gender roles as men being hunters and women being gatherers is being challenged by recent findings and research. This new evidence suggests that women were not just gatherers but also active participants in hunting activities. These discoveries are transforming our understanding of prehistoric societies and highlighting the importance of recognizing the egalitarian nature of our ancient ancestors.

1.2.1 Shifting Paradigms

For many years, the prevailing assumption was that men were the primary hunters in prehistoric societies, while women played a secondary role as gatherers. This assumption was based on limited evidence and biased interpretations of archaeological findings. However, as our understanding of prehistoric cultures deepens and new research methods emerge, a more nuanced picture is emerging.

1.2.2 Archaeological and Anthropological Evidence

Archaeological and anthropological studies have revealed a wealth of evidence that challenges the traditional gender roles in prehistoric societies. Excavations at various sites have uncovered tools and weapons associated with hunting activities, such as projectile points and animal remains, in close proximity to female burials. These findings suggest that women were actively involved in hunting and not just passive gatherers.

1.2.3 Ethnographic Comparisons

Ethnographic studies of contemporary hunter-gatherer societies provide further support for the idea that women played a significant role in hunting. These societies, which have been studied for their similarities to prehistoric cultures, often show a more egalitarian division of labor between men and women. Women are frequently involved in hunting activities, contributing to the group's food procurement and overall survival.

1.2.4 Biological Factors

Biological factors also support the idea that women were hunters in prehistoric societies. Studies have shown that women possess physical attributes, such as endurance and fine motor skills, that are essential for successful hunting. Additionally, the presence of female-specific hunting tools, such as traps and snares, further suggests that women actively participated in hunting activities.

1.2.5 Social Implications

The recognition of women as hunters in prehistoric societies has significant social implications. It challenges the long-held assumption that men were the dominant figures in early human societies and highlights the egalitarian nature of our ancient ancestors. This new understanding of prehistoric gender roles has the potential to reshape our perceptions of gender equality and challenge modern gender norms.

1.2.6 The Evolution of Gender Roles

The evolution of gender roles in prehistoric societies is a complex and multifaceted process. It is influenced by a combination of biological, social, and cultural factors. The recognition of women as hunters suggests that gender roles were not fixed but evolved over time in response to changing environmental and social conditions.

1.2.7 The Importance of Challenging Assumptions

Challenging assumptions about prehistoric gender roles is crucial for a more accurate understanding of our ancient ancestors. By questioning long-held beliefs and biases, we can uncover the diverse and complex ways in which early humans lived and interacted. This new perspective allows us to appreciate the contributions of women in prehistoric societies and challenges the notion that gender roles have always been rigidly defined.

1.2.8 Opening New Avenues for Research

The recognition of women as hunters opens up new avenues for research into the lives of our ancient ancestors. It prompts us to reevaluate existing archaeological evidence and explore new methods of analysis. By focusing on the activities and roles of women in prehistoric societies, we can gain a more comprehensive understanding of their daily lives, social dynamics, and contributions to their communities.

1.2.9 Conclusion

The evolution of gender roles in prehistoric societies is a complex and dynamic process. Recent research and evidence challenge the conventional portrayal of men as hunters and women as gatherers. The recognition of women as hunters highlights the egalitarian nature of our ancient ancestors and opens up new avenues for research. By challenging assumptions and biases, we can gain a more accurate understanding of prehistoric gender roles and their implications for modern society.

1.3 The Significance of Challenging Assumptions

The conventional portrayal of prehistoric gender roles has long depicted men as hunters and women as gatherers, perpetuating the notion that women played a passive role in early human societies. However, recent research and archaeological findings have challenged this assumption, revealing a more complex and nuanced understanding of prehistoric gender dynamics. This shift in perspective not only reshapes our understanding of our ancient ancestors but also has broader implications for our understanding of human evolution and the development of gender roles in society.

1.3.1 Reevaluating Prehistoric Gender Roles

The discovery of evidence suggesting that women were hunters challenges the traditional narrative of prehistoric gender roles. Archaeological excavations have unearthed tools and weapons associated with hunting activities in female burial sites, indicating that women actively participated in hunting. These findings challenge the notion that hunting was exclusively a male domain and highlight the need to reevaluate preconceived notions about gender roles in prehistoric societies.

1.3.2 Expanding the Scope of Research

By challenging assumptions about prehistoric gender roles, we open up new avenues for research into the lives of our ancient ancestors. This shift in perspective encourages scholars to explore previously unconsidered aspects of prehistoric societies, such as the division of labor, social organization, and the dynamics of power and decision-making. It prompts us to question the biases and limitations of previous research and encourages a more inclusive and comprehensive understanding of our shared human history.

1.3.3 Understanding Human Evolution

The significance of challenging assumptions about prehistoric gender roles extends beyond the realm of archaeology. It has profound implications for our understanding of human evolution and the development of gender roles in society. The traditional view of men as hunters and women as gatherers has often been used to support the argument that gender differences are biologically determined and rooted in our evolutionary past. However, the discovery of female hunters challenges this notion, suggesting that gender roles were not fixed but rather shaped by social and cultural factors.

1.3.4 Egalitarianism in Prehistoric Societies

The recognition of women as hunters in prehistoric societies provides evidence of a more egalitarian social structure. It suggests that early human communities may have operated on principles of cooperation, where both men and women contributed to the survival and well-being of the group. This egalitarianism challenges the assumption that gender inequality is a natural or inherent aspect of human societies and highlights the potential for more equitable social structures.

1.3.5 Challenging Gender Stereotypes

Challenging assumptions about prehistoric gender roles also has implications for modern society. It prompts us to question the gender stereotypes and biases that persist in contemporary culture and challenges the notion that certain roles or activities are inherently gendered. By recognizing the historical presence of female hunters, we challenge the limitations imposed by gender norms and open up possibilities for greater gender equality and empowerment in the present.

1.3.6 Inspiring Future Research

The significance of challenging assumptions about prehistoric gender roles lies in its potential to inspire future research and exploration. By acknowledging the presence and contributions of female hunters in our ancient past, we encourage further investigation into the lives and experiences of women in prehistoric societies. This research can shed light on the diversity of human experiences and challenge the notion of a single, dominant narrative of human history.

1.3.7 A More Inclusive Understanding of Prehistoric Gender Roles

In conclusion, the significance of challenging assumptions about prehistoric gender roles cannot be overstated. It not only reshapes our understanding of our ancient ancestors but also has broader implications for our understanding of human evolution, the development of gender roles, and the potential for more equitable societies. By recognizing the presence of female hunters, we challenge long-held assumptions, expand the scope of research, and inspire a more inclusive understanding of prehistoric gender roles. This shift in perspective invites us to reimagine our shared human history and consider the diverse contributions of both men and women in shaping our past and present.

1.4 Research Methodology and Sources

In order to explore the role of women as hunters in prehistoric societies, it is crucial to employ a rigorous research methodology and draw from a diverse range of sources. This chapter will outline the research methods utilized in this book and provide an overview of the sources that have contributed to our understanding of ancient huntresses.

1.4.1 Archaeological Research

Archaeology plays a fundamental role in uncovering the material remains of past societies. Through the excavation and analysis of artifacts, structures, and human remains, archaeologists can piece together the lives and activities of ancient peoples. In the context of studying female hunters, archaeological research has been instrumental in providing tangible evidence of their existence.

Excavations at various archaeological sites have unearthed tools and weapons associated with hunting activities. These artifacts, such as projectile points, spearheads, and animal bone fragments with cut marks, provide direct evidence of hunting practices. By examining the distribution and frequency of these hunting-related artifacts, researchers can gain insights into the participation of women in hunting activities.

1.4.2 Ethnographic Studies

Ethnographic studies of contemporary hunter-gatherer societies have also contributed significantly to our understanding of prehistoric gender roles. By observing and interacting with these societies, researchers can gain insights into the gender dynamics and division of labor within hunting and gathering activities. Ethnographic studies have revealed that in many hunter-gatherer societies, women actively participate in hunting alongside men, challenging the notion that hunting was exclusively a male domain.

1.4.3 Paleontological Evidence

Paleontological research, focusing on the study of ancient animal remains, has provided valuable insights into the behaviors and interactions of early humans. By examining the fossilized remains of animals hunted by our ancestors, researchers can infer the hunting strategies and techniques employed. Additionally, the analysis of dental wear patterns and isotopic analysis of ancient human remains can shed light on the diet and nutritional patterns of prehistoric populations, further supporting the role of hunting in their survival.

1.4.4 Comparative Studies

Comparative studies, which involve analyzing data from multiple archaeological sites and time periods, have allowed researchers to identify patterns and trends in prehistoric gender roles. By examining the presence of hunting-related artifacts and the distribution of gender-specific grave goods, researchers can discern variations in gender roles across different societies and time periods. These comparative studies provide a broader perspective on the prevalence and significance of female hunters in prehistoric societies.

1.4.5 Interdisciplinary Approaches

Recognizing the complexity of studying prehistoric gender roles, interdisciplinary approaches have become increasingly important. By integrating insights from various disciplines such as archaeology, anthropology, paleontology, and gender studies, researchers can develop a more comprehensive understanding of ancient huntresses. These interdisciplinary collaborations allow for a more nuanced interpretation of the available evidence and facilitate the exploration of new research questions.

1.4.6 Limitations and Challenges

It is important to acknowledge the limitations and challenges inherent in studying prehistoric gender roles. The scarcity of direct evidence and the biases present in archaeological interpretations can pose significant obstacles. Additionally, the interpretation of artifacts and the reconstruction of ancient behaviors are subject to the biases and assumptions of the researchers involved. It is crucial to approach the study of ancient huntresses with a critical and self-reflective mindset, constantly questioning our own biases and assumptions.

1.4.7 Conclusion

The research methodology employed in this book combines archaeological research, ethnographic studies, paleontological evidence, comparative studies, and interdisciplinary approaches. By drawing from a diverse range of sources, we aim to present a comprehensive and balanced understanding of the role of women as hunters in prehistoric societies. Through this multidisciplinary approach, we can challenge long-held assumptions and contribute to a more inclusive understanding of prehistoric gender roles.

2

Chapter 2

The Huntress Unmasked

2.1 Archaeological Evidence of Female Hunters

The conventional understanding of prehistoric gender roles has long portrayed men as hunters and women as gatherers, with men taking on the role of the primary food providers while women stayed closer to home, tending to domestic tasks and childcare. However, recent archaeological findings have challenged this narrative, providing compelling evidence that women were not just gatherers but also active participants in hunting activities. This new research has revolutionized our understanding of prehistoric societies and sheds light on the complex dynamics of early human communities.

2.1.1 The Shift in Archaeological Interpretations

Archaeological excavations have unearthed a wealth of evidence that challenges the traditional view of gender roles in prehistoric societies. The discovery of ancient hunting tools, such as spears and projectile points, in close proximity to female remains has raised questions about the extent of women's involvement in hunting activities. These findings suggest that women played a more active role in procuring food for their communities than previously believed.

2.1.2 Burial Sites and Funerary Practices

Another significant source of evidence comes from the analysis of burial sites and funerary practices. In many prehistoric societies, grave goods were commonly included in burials as offerings for the afterlife. The presence of hunting-related artifacts, such as animal bones, hunting tools, and even depictions of hunting scenes on pottery or cave walls, alongside female burials, suggests that women were intimately connected to hunting practices. These findings challenge the notion that hunting was exclusively a male domain and indicate a more egalitarian division of labor within these ancient societies.

2.1.3 Rock Art and Cave Paintings

Rock art and cave paintings provide a fascinating glimpse into the lives of our ancient ancestors. These artistic representations often depict scenes of hunting, with both men and women actively engaged in the pursuit of game. The presence of female figures in these hunting scenes suggests that women not only participated in hunting but also held a significant role in these activities. These visual records challenge the traditional narrative of gender roles and provide tangible evidence of the active involvement of women in hunting practices.

2.1.4 Analysis of Animal Remains

The analysis of animal remains found at archaeological sites has also contributed to our understanding of prehistoric gender roles. By examining the distribution of different animal species and their age profiles, researchers can gain insights into hunting strategies and the involvement of different members of the community. Studies have shown that women were not only involved in hunting but also played a crucial role in the procurement of small game, which was essential for the survival of early human communities.

2.1.5 Ethnographic Studies and Indigenous Knowledge

In addition to archaeological evidence, ethnographic studies of contemporary hunter-gatherer societies have provided valuable insights into the role of women in hunting. Many indigenous communities around the world have maintained traditional hunting practices, offering a window into the past. These studies reveal that women often participate in hunting activities, contributing to the overall food security of their communities. The knowledge and skills passed down through generations challenge the notion that hunting was exclusively a male endeavor.

2.1.6 The Importance of Contextualizing Evidence

While the archaeological evidence of female hunters is compelling, it is crucial to interpret these findings within their cultural and environmental contexts. The roles and responsibilities of women in hunting may have varied across different regions and time periods, influenced by factors such as resource availability, social organization, and technological advancements. It is essential to consider these factors when reconstructing the lives of ancient huntresses and understanding the complexities of prehistoric gender roles.

In conclusion, the archaeological evidence of female hunters challenges long-held assumptions about prehistoric gender roles. The discovery of hunting tools, the analysis of burial sites, the examination of rock art, and the study of animal remains all contribute to a more nuanced understanding of the active participation of women in hunting activities. By recognizing the significant role of women as hunters, we gain a deeper appreciation for the egalitarian nature of early human societies. This newfound understanding not only reshapes our perception of the past but also has implications for modern gender equality and the recognition of women's contributions throughout history.

2.2 Paleontological Discoveries and Their Implications

Paleontological discoveries have played a crucial role in reshaping our understanding of prehistoric gender roles. These findings have challenged the traditional notion that men were the sole hunters while women remained primarily as gatherers. Instead, they provide compelling evidence that women were active participants in hunting activities, contributing significantly to the survival and success of early human communities.

2.2.1 Fossil Evidence of Female Hunters

One of the most significant paleontological discoveries supporting the presence of female hunters is the identification of female skeletal remains with hunting-related injuries. These injuries include fractures, bone deformities, and embedded projectile points, indicating direct involvement in hunting activities. For many years, these injuries were often attributed to male hunters, but recent studies have shown that a significant number of these injuries were sustained by females.

Furthermore, the analysis of fossilized teeth has provided valuable insights into the diet of ancient humans. The presence of wear patterns consistent with the use of hunting tools suggests that women were actively engaged in processing and consuming meat. This challenges the notion that women were solely responsible for gathering plant-based foods and highlights their role as skilled hunters.

2.2.2 Hunting Tools and Technology

Paleontological evidence has also revealed the presence of hunting tools associated with female remains. Excavations have uncovered projectile points, spearheads, and other hunting implements in close proximity to female skeletons. These findings indicate that women not only participated in hunting but also possessed the necessary tools and technology to effectively engage in these activities.

The discovery of these hunting tools also raises questions about the division of labor within prehistoric societies. It suggests that gender roles were not as rigidly defined as previously believed, and that women had the agency to engage in activities traditionally associated with men.

2.2.3 Hunting Strategies and Adaptations

Paleontological research has shed light on the hunting strategies employed by ancient humans, further supporting the involvement of women in hunting. Studies of fossilized animal remains have revealed patterns consistent with cooperative hunting, where individuals worked together to capture large game. This cooperative hunting behavior is seen in both male and female remains, indicating that women played an active role in group hunts.

Additionally, the analysis of ancient footprints has provided valuable insights into the physical capabilities of female hunters. These footprints show evidence of running, tracking, and stalking, suggesting that women possessed the necessary physical adaptations for successful hunting.

2.2.4 The Implications of Paleontological Discoveries

The paleontological discoveries discussed above have significant implications for our understanding of prehistoric gender roles. They challenge the long-held assumption that men were the primary hunters, while women were confined to gathering activities. Instead, they suggest that early human societies were more egalitarian, with both men and women actively participating in hunting and gathering.

These findings also highlight the importance of recognizing the diverse roles and contributions of women in prehistoric societies. By acknowledging the presence of female hunters, we gain a more comprehensive understanding of the complexity and diversity of early human communities. This recognition also challenges modern gender stereotypes and provides a historical precedent for gender equality.

Furthermore, the implications of these discoveries extend beyond the realm of gender studies. They have broader implications for our understanding of human evolution, social dynamics, and the development of complex societies. By recognizing the active participation of women in hunting, we gain a deeper appreciation for the cooperative nature of early human communities and the importance of shared responsibilities in ensuring survival and success.

In conclusion, paleontological discoveries have played a crucial role in reshaping our understanding of prehistoric gender roles. The evidence of female hunters challenges traditional assumptions and provides a more inclusive and egalitarian perspective on early human societies. These discoveries not only highlight the active participation of women in hunting activities but also have broader implications for our understanding of human evolution and the importance of cooperation in early human communities.

2.3 Anthropological Studies on Female Hunting

Anthropological studies have played a crucial role in unraveling the truth about prehistoric gender roles and challenging the conventional assumptions that have long portrayed men as hunters and women as gatherers. These studies have provided valuable insights into the lives of our ancient ancestors, revealing a more egalitarian society where women played a significant role as hunters.

2.3.1 The Shift in Anthropological Perspectives

Anthropologists have long recognized the importance of studying gender roles in understanding the dynamics of ancient societies. However, it is only in recent years that the focus has shifted towards reevaluating prehistoric gender roles and challenging the traditional narrative. This shift has been driven by the discovery of new archaeological evidence and the application of more inclusive research methodologies.

2.3.2 Ethnographic Studies of Hunter-Gatherer Societies

One of the key sources of evidence for female hunting comes from the study of contemporary hunter-gatherer societies. Ethnographic studies have revealed that in many of these societies, women actively participate in hunting activities alongside men. This suggests that the division of labor based on gender roles observed in modern societies may not accurately reflect prehistoric realities.

2.3.3 Analysis of Ancient Artifacts

Anthropologists have also turned to the analysis of ancient artifacts to gain insights into the roles of women in hunting. By examining tools and weapons found in archaeological sites, researchers have been able to identify traces of use-wear patterns that indicate the involvement of women in hunting activities. These findings challenge the notion that hunting was exclusively a male domain.

2.3.4 Examination of Human Skeletal Remains

The study of human skeletal remains has provided further evidence of female hunting in prehistoric societies. Anthropologists have analyzed the physical characteristics of ancient individuals to determine their roles in hunting and gathering. The presence of injuries consistent with hunting activities in female skeletons suggests that women actively participated in hunting and were exposed to the same risks as their male counterparts.

2.3.5 Cross-Cultural Studies

Anthropologists have also conducted cross-cultural studies to compare gender roles in different societies throughout history. By examining a wide range of cultures, researchers have identified patterns that challenge the assumption of male dominance in hunting. These studies have revealed that in many societies, women played a crucial role in providing food through hunting, challenging the notion that hunting was solely a male activity.

2.3.6 Oral Traditions and Indigenous Knowledge

In addition to archaeological and anthropological evidence, researchers have also turned to oral traditions and indigenous knowledge to gain insights into prehistoric gender roles. Many indigenous communities have preserved stories and cultural practices that highlight the involvement of women in hunting. These narratives provide valuable perspectives on the historical realities of female hunting and challenge the biases inherent in Western interpretations of prehistory.

2.3.7 The Importance of Interdisciplinary Approaches

Anthropological studies on female hunting have highlighted the importance of interdisciplinary approaches in understanding prehistoric gender roles. Collaboration between archaeologists, anthropologists, historians, and other experts has allowed for a more comprehensive analysis of the available evidence. By combining different methodologies and perspectives, researchers have been able to challenge long-held assumptions and develop a more nuanced understanding of prehistoric societies.

2.3.8 Implications for Our Understanding of Prehistoric Gender Roles

The anthropological studies on female hunting have significant implications for our understanding of prehistoric gender roles. They challenge the traditional narrative that portrays men as the primary hunters and women as passive gatherers. Instead, they reveal a more complex and egalitarian society where women actively participated in hunting activities. This challenges the notion of fixed gender roles and highlights the diversity of human experiences throughout history.

2.3.9 Opening New Avenues for Research

The recognition of female hunting in prehistoric societies has opened up new avenues for research. Anthropologists are now exploring the social dynamics of hunting groups, the impact of female hunters on group dynamics, and the role of women in leadership and decision-making within these groups. These studies not only contribute to our understanding of prehistoric societies but also shed light on the evolution of human social structures and the origins of gender roles.

In conclusion, anthropological studies have played a crucial role in challenging the conventional assumptions about prehistoric gender roles. By examining a wide range of evidence, including ethnographic studies, analysis of ancient artifacts, examination of human skeletal remains, cross-cultural comparisons, and indigenous knowledge, researchers have revealed the active participation of women in hunting activities. These studies have not only transformed our understanding of prehistoric societies but also highlighted the importance of interdisciplinary approaches and the need to challenge long-held assumptions in archaeological research.

2.4 Reconstructing the Lives of Ancient Huntresses

The discovery of female hunters in prehistoric societies has revolutionized our understanding of ancient gender roles. As we delve deeper into the lives of our ancient ancestors, it becomes increasingly clear that women played a significant role in hunting, challenging the traditional notion that they were solely gatherers confined to the domestic sphere. In this chapter, we will explore the various methods and approaches used to reconstruct the lives of these ancient huntresses, shedding light on their contributions to early human societies.

2.4.1 Archaeological Clues

Archaeological evidence provides valuable insights into the lives of ancient huntresses. Excavations at various sites have unearthed tools and artifacts associated with hunting activities, such as projectile points, spearheads, and animal remains. By analyzing these artifacts, researchers can determine the gender of the individuals who used them. For instance, the discovery of female skeletons buried with hunting implements suggests their active participation in hunting.

Furthermore, the spatial distribution of artifacts within archaeological sites can provide clues about the division of labor between men and women. If hunting tools are found in areas traditionally associated with male activities, such as hunting camps or communal spaces, it suggests that women were actively involved in hunting alongside men. This challenges the notion that hunting was exclusively a male domain.

2.4.2 Ethnographic Studies

Ethnographic studies of modern hunter-gatherer societies have also contributed to our understanding of ancient huntresses. By observing and interacting with these societies, researchers gain valuable insights into the roles and responsibilities of women in hunting activities. Many contemporary hunter-gatherer societies exhibit gender egalitarianism, where women actively participate in hunting alongside men.

These studies reveal that women possess extensive knowledge of local flora and fauna, making them skilled hunters. They often employ different hunting techniques and strategies compared to men, utilizing their unique strengths and abilities. By examining these modern practices, we can infer that similar dynamics may have existed in prehistoric societies, where women played an integral role in securing food resources.

2.4.3 Paleoenvironmental Reconstructions

Paleoenvironmental reconstructions provide another avenue for understanding the lives of ancient huntresses. By analyzing fossilized pollen, plant remains, and animal bones, researchers can reconstruct the environments in which our ancestors lived. This information helps us understand the availability and distribution of resources, including the types of animals that were hunted.

By examining the remains of large game animals, researchers can determine the hunting strategies employed by ancient societies. If the remains of these animals are found in close proximity to archaeological sites associated with women, it suggests their involvement in hunting. Additionally, the presence of specialized hunting tools, such as traps or snares, further supports the hypothesis of female hunters.

2.4.4 Comparative Studies

Comparative studies across different cultures and time periods provide a broader perspective on the role of ancient huntresses. By examining the similarities and differences in gender roles and hunting practices, researchers can identify patterns and trends. These studies reveal that the participation of women in hunting activities is not limited to a specific time or region but is a recurring theme throughout human history.

Comparative studies also highlight the cultural and social factors that influence the division of labor between men and women. In some societies, women may have played a more prominent role in hunting, while in others, their involvement may have been more limited. By understanding these variations, we can gain a more nuanced understanding of the complex dynamics of ancient gender roles.

2.4.5 Interdisciplinary Approaches

Reconstructing the lives of ancient huntresses requires an interdisciplinary approach that combines archaeological, anthropological, and paleoenvironmental research. By integrating data from various fields, researchers can paint a more comprehensive picture of the lives of these ancient women. This collaborative effort allows for a more accurate interpretation of the available evidence and helps overcome biases and limitations inherent in individual disciplines.

Furthermore, interdisciplinary research enables us to explore the broader implications of female hunting in prehistoric societies. It allows us to examine the impact of gender roles on social dynamics, decision-making processes, and the overall survival and success of early human groups. By considering these factors, we can gain a deeper appreciation for the contributions of ancient huntresses and their significance in shaping our evolutionary history.

In conclusion, reconstructing the lives of ancient huntresses is a complex and multifaceted endeavor. Through archaeological evidence, ethnographic studies, paleoenvironmental reconstructions, comparative analysis, and interdisciplinary approaches, we are gradually unraveling the truth about prehistoric gender roles. The evidence overwhelmingly supports the active participation of women in hunting activities, challenging long-held assumptions and providing a more inclusive understanding of our ancient ancestors. By recognizing the important role of ancient huntresses, we gain valuable insights into the egalitarian nature of early human societies and the diverse contributions of both men and women to our evolutionary journey.

3

Chapter 3

Hunting Techniques and Tools

3.1 Weapons and Hunting Implements

The study of prehistoric gender roles has traditionally depicted men as the primary hunters, while women were relegated to the role of gatherers. However, recent archaeological and anthropological research has challenged this long-held assumption, revealing that women played a significant role as hunters in ancient societies. In this chapter, we will explore the weapons and hunting implements used by these ancient huntresses, shedding light on their hunting techniques and the tools they employed.

3.1.1 Stone Tools: The Foundation of Hunting

Stone tools were the foundation of hunting for our ancient ancestors, and women were no exception in utilizing these implements. The development and refinement of stone tools played a crucial role in the success of hunting endeavors. Women, like men, would have crafted and used various types of stone tools, such as spears, knives, and scrapers, to aid in their hunting activities.

Spears were one of the most important weapons used by ancient huntresses.

These weapons were typically made from sharpened wooden shafts with stone or bone tips. The design and construction of these spears allowed for effective thrusting and throwing, enabling women to engage in both close-range and long-range hunting.

Knives and scrapers were also essential tools for hunting. These implements were used for skinning and butchering animals, as well as for preparing hides and other materials for clothing and shelter. The ability to efficiently process animal carcasses was crucial for survival in prehistoric times, and women would have played a vital role in these tasks.

3.1.2 Projectile Weapons: Enhancing Hunting Efficiency

In addition to stone tools, ancient huntresses also utilized various projectile weapons to enhance their hunting efficiency. These weapons allowed for hunting from a distance, reducing the risk of injury and increasing the chances of a successful hunt.

One such projectile weapon used by ancient huntresses was the atlatl. The atlatl was a spear-throwing device that provided greater speed and accuracy when throwing spears. By using the atlatl, women could effectively hunt larger game from a safer distance, increasing their chances of a successful kill.

Another important projectile weapon used by ancient huntresses was the bow and arrow. The invention of the bow and arrow revolutionized hunting techniques, allowing for even greater accuracy and range. Women would have honed their skills in archery, enabling them to participate in group hunts and contribute to the overall success of the hunting party.

3.1.3 Traps and Snares: Cunning Hunting Techniques

Ancient huntresses also employed various traps and snares to capture animals. These hunting techniques required careful planning, knowledge of animal behavior, and skillful execution. Women would have utilized their understanding of the natural environment and animal behavior to set up effective traps and snares.

Pitfall traps were commonly used by ancient huntresses. These traps involved digging deep holes and covering them with branches and leaves to camouflage them. When an animal unknowingly stepped on the trap, it would fall into the pit, making it easier for women to capture and kill the animal.

Snares were another effective hunting technique employed by ancient huntresses. These consisted of loops made from plant fibers or animal sinew, strategically placed to ensnare animals as they moved through their natural habitats. Women would have set up snares in areas frequented by game, increasing their chances of a successful hunt.

3.1.4 Adapting to Different Environments

The weapons and hunting implements used by ancient huntresses were not limited to a specific environment. These resourceful women adapted their hunting techniques and tools to various landscapes and ecosystems.

In open grasslands, where long-range hunting was necessary, the use of spears and projectile weapons like the atlatl and bow and arrow would have been prevalent. In forested areas, where close-range hunting was more common, women would have relied on spears and stone tools for hunting.

The ability of ancient huntresses to adapt their hunting techniques and tools to different environments demonstrates their resourcefulness and versatility as hunters. It also challenges the notion that women were solely confined to the role of gatherers, highlighting their active participation in hunting activities.

In conclusion, the weapons and hunting implements used by ancient huntresses were diverse and varied. From stone tools to projectile weapons and cunning traps, these women utilized a range of tools and techniques to contribute to the success of hunting endeavors. The evidence of their active participation in hunting challenges traditional gender roles and provides a more inclusive understanding of prehistoric societies. By recognizing the significant role of women as hunters, we gain a deeper appreciation for the egalitarian nature of our ancient ancestors and the importance of challenging long-held assumptions about prehistoric gender roles.

3.2 Hunting Strategies and Tactics

Hunting was a crucial activity for early humans, providing them with a vital source of food and resources. The strategies and tactics employed by ancient huntresses were diverse and adaptable, reflecting the different environments they inhabited and the prey they pursued. This section explores the hunting strategies and tactics employed by women in prehistoric times, shedding light on their remarkable skills and contributions to group survival.

3.2.1 Cooperative Hunting

Cooperative hunting was a common practice among early humans, and women played a significant role in these group endeavors. The huntresses would collaborate with other members of their community, including men, to plan and execute successful hunts. This cooperative approach allowed for the pooling of knowledge, skills, and resources, maximizing the chances of a successful outcome.

In cooperative hunting, women would often take on specific roles based on their strengths and abilities. While men may have been physically stronger and better suited for certain tasks, such as throwing spears or engaging in close combat, women brought their own unique skills to the table. They were often adept at tracking and stalking prey, utilizing their keen observational skills and knowledge of animal behavior to their advantage.

3.2.2 Ambush and Stealth

One of the key hunting strategies employed by ancient huntresses was ambush and stealth. Women would carefully observe their surroundings, identifying potential prey and studying their habits and patterns. They would then plan their approach, using natural cover and terrain to conceal their presence and get as close to the prey as possible.

The ability to move silently and remain undetected was crucial for a successful ambush. Women would employ various techniques to minimize noise and avoid alerting their quarry, such as moving slowly and deliberately, avoiding stepping on dry leaves or twigs, and using hand signals to communicate with their hunting partners.

3.2.3 Persistence Hunting

Persistence hunting was another hunting strategy employed by ancient huntresses, particularly in open landscapes where prey had limited opportunities for cover. This technique involved tracking and pursuing prey over long distances until the animal became exhausted and could no longer flee.

Women would utilize their endurance and stamina to their advantage during persistence hunts. They would carefully track the prey, maintaining a steady pace and conserving energy while gradually closing the distance. By persistently following the animal, they would eventually wear it down, leading to a successful kill.

3.2.4 Trapping and Netting

In addition to direct hunting, ancient huntresses also employed trapping and netting techniques to capture prey. Traps were constructed using natural materials such as branches, stones, and vines, strategically placed to ensnare or immobilize animals. Netting involved the use of woven nets made from plant fibers or animal sinew, which could be set up in strategic locations to catch or entangle prey.

Women would use their knowledge of animal behavior and movement patterns to determine the most effective locations for setting traps or deploying nets. These techniques allowed for the capture of smaller game, such as birds, rabbits, and fish, which could supplement the diet of the community.

3.2.5 Adaptation to Different Environments

The hunting strategies and tactics employed by ancient huntresses varied depending on the environment in which they lived. In open grasslands, persistence hunting and ambush techniques were more prevalent, taking advantage of the lack of cover for prey. In forested areas, where concealment was easier, ambush and trapping techniques were more commonly used.

The ability of ancient huntresses to adapt their hunting strategies to different environments demonstrates their resourcefulness and adaptability. It also highlights their deep understanding of the natural world and their ability to exploit its resources effectively.

3.2.6 The Role of Women in Group Hunts

Women played a crucial role in group hunts, contributing their unique skills and knowledge to ensure the success of the endeavor. Their participation in hunting not only provided valuable resources for the community but also fostered social cohesion and cooperation among group members.

The involvement of women in hunting groups challenged traditional gender roles and fostered a more egalitarian society. The recognition of women as skilled hunters and contributors to group survival shattered long-held assumptions about prehistoric gender roles and highlighted the importance of a more inclusive understanding of our ancient ancestors.

By examining the hunting strategies and tactics employed by ancient huntresses, we gain a deeper appreciation for their skills, intelligence, and resourcefulness. Their contributions to group survival were essential, and their ability to adapt to different environments and employ diverse hunting techniques showcases the remarkable capabilities of early human societies.

As we continue to challenge and reassess prehistoric gender roles, it is crucial to recognize the significant role that women played in hunting and the impact it had on the social dynamics of early human communities. By acknowledging the hunting legacies of our ancient huntresses, we can gain valuable insights into the complexity and diversity of prehistoric societies, ultimately leading to a more inclusive understanding of our shared human history.

3.3 Hunting in Different Environments

Hunting was a crucial activity for early humans, providing them with food, resources, and a means of survival. As we explore the role of women in hunting, it is essential to consider the diverse environments in which our ancient ancestors lived and adapted their hunting techniques. This chapter delves into the various environments in which women hunted, highlighting their adaptability and resourcefulness.

3.3.1 Forests and Woodlands

Forests and woodlands were abundant environments that provided a diverse range of prey for early humans. Women, as skilled hunters, navigated these dense landscapes with agility and precision. They developed strategies to track and ambush their targets, utilizing their knowledge of the terrain and the behavior of their prey.

In these environments, women employed various hunting techniques. They used bows and arrows, crafted from materials found in the forest, to silently take down their quarry from a distance. Additionally, they utilized traps and snares strategically placed along game trails, ensuring a higher chance of success in capturing animals.

The forest and woodland environments demanded a deep understanding of the ecosystem and the behavior of different species. Women honed their skills in observation, recognizing patterns and signs that indicated the presence of prey. They also developed an intimate knowledge of the plants and herbs in these environments, utilizing them for medicinal purposes and enhancing their hunting abilities.

3.3.2 Grasslands and Savannas

Grasslands and savannas presented a different set of challenges and opportunities for women hunters. These open landscapes provided visibility and allowed for the pursuit of fast-moving prey. Women adapted their hunting techniques to these environments, employing both individual and group hunting strategies.

In the grasslands, women often engaged in persistence hunting, a technique that involved tracking and chasing prey over long distances until the animal exhausted itself. This required exceptional endurance and stamina, skills that women possessed in abundance. By utilizing their knowledge of the terrain and the behavior of the animals, they were able to outlast their prey and secure a successful hunt.

Group hunting was also prevalent in grassland and savanna environments. Women collaborated with other members of their community, employing coordinated tactics to surround and capture larger game. This cooperative approach allowed for the efficient utilization of resources and increased the chances of a successful hunt.

3.3.3 Mountains and Highlands

Mountains and highlands presented unique challenges for women hunters. These rugged terrains required physical strength, endurance, and adaptability. Women developed specialized hunting techniques to navigate these environments and secure valuable resources.

In mountainous regions, women often engaged in stalking and ambush hunting. They utilized their knowledge of the landscape and the behavior of their prey to position themselves strategically, ensuring a successful kill. Additionally, they employed throwing spears and other long-range weapons to overcome the challenges posed by the steep and treacherous terrain.

The mountainous environments also provided opportunities for women to hunt smaller game, such as birds and small mammals. They utilized traps, nets, and snares to capture these elusive creatures, showcasing their resourcefulness and adaptability in diverse hunting scenarios.

3.3.4 Coastal and Aquatic Environments

Coastal and aquatic environments offered a rich source of food and resources for early humans. Women played a significant role in hunting marine life, showcasing their ability to adapt to different environments and exploit available resources.

In coastal regions, women employed various fishing techniques, including netting, spearfishing, and the use of traps. They developed an understanding of the tides, currents, and migratory patterns of marine species, allowing them to maximize their catch. Women also utilized boats and rafts, enabling them to venture further into the water and access a wider range of prey.

In addition to fishing, women in coastal environments engaged in hunting marine mammals, such as seals and dolphins. They crafted specialized weapons, such as harpoons and throwing spears, to overcome the challenges posed by these formidable creatures. The ability to hunt in coastal and aquatic environments provided early humans with a diverse and reliable source of food, contributing to their survival and development.

3.3.5 Desert and Arid Environments

Desert and arid environments presented unique challenges for women hunters. These harsh landscapes required specialized knowledge and skills to navigate and secure resources. Women adapted their hunting techniques to these environments, showcasing their resilience and ingenuity.

In desert regions, women often engaged in tracking and stalking techniques to locate and capture elusive prey. They utilized their knowledge of the desert's flora and fauna, recognizing the subtle signs that indicated the presence of animals. Additionally, they employed stealth and patience to approach their targets undetected, ensuring a successful hunt.

Water sources were scarce in desert environments, making them critical hunting grounds. Women developed techniques to trap and capture animals near these vital resources, maximizing their chances of securing food and sustenance. They also utilized their knowledge of edible plants and insects, supplementing their diet and ensuring their survival in these challenging environments.

Conclusion

The diverse environments in which women hunted highlight their adaptability, resourcefulness, and deep understanding of the natural world. From forests and grasslands to mountains and coastal regions, women developed specialized hunting techniques to secure food and resources for their communities. By recognizing the significant role of women in hunting across various environments, we gain a more comprehensive understanding of prehistoric gender roles and the egalitarian nature of early human societies.

3.4 The Role of Women in Group Hunts

Throughout history, the prevailing assumption has been that men were the primary hunters in prehistoric societies, while women played a secondary role as gatherers. However, recent research and archaeological findings have challenged this traditional view, shedding light on the significant role that women played as hunters in ancient societies. This chapter explores the role of women in group hunts, highlighting their contributions, strategies, and the implications of their participation.

3.4.1 Women as Skilled Hunters

Contrary to popular belief, women in prehistoric societies were not limited to gathering activities. They actively participated in group hunts, displaying remarkable hunting skills and contributing to the survival of their communities. Archaeological evidence has revealed the presence of female hunters through the discovery of hunting tools and weapons associated with women. These findings suggest that women were not only capable of hunting but also actively engaged in it.

3.4.2 The Division of Labor in Group Hunts

In group hunts, women played a crucial role in complementing the skills of their male counterparts. While men often focused on larger game, women specialized in hunting smaller animals, such as birds, rabbits, and small mammals. This division of labor allowed for a more efficient and successful hunt, as different prey required different hunting techniques and strategies. Women's expertise in hunting smaller game contributed to the overall food resources of the community and ensured a diverse and balanced diet.

3.4.3 Cooperative Hunting Strategies

Group hunts required coordination, cooperation, and effective communication among hunters. Women played an integral role in these endeavors, contributing to the success of the hunt through their knowledge and skills. They actively participated in planning and strategizing, sharing their expertise in tracking, trapping, and ambushing prey. The ability to work together as a cohesive unit was essential for the survival of the group, and women's involvement in group hunts played a significant role in ensuring the success of these endeavors.

3.4.4 Women as Providers and Nurturers

The participation of women in group hunts went beyond the acquisition of food. It also had social and cultural implications. By actively contributing to the hunt, women demonstrated their ability to provide for their families and communities. This challenged the notion that men were the sole providers and highlighted the importance of women's contributions to the overall well-being of the group. Additionally, women's involvement in hunting allowed them to pass down valuable knowledge and skills to future generations, ensuring the continuity of hunting traditions.

3.4.5 The Significance of Women's Participation

The inclusion of women in group hunts had profound implications for prehistoric societies. It fostered a sense of equality and cooperation among community members, challenging the notion of rigid gender roles. The recognition of women as skilled hunters and providers contributed to a more egalitarian society, where both men and women played essential roles in the survival and prosperity of the group. This egalitarianism extended beyond hunting activities and likely influenced other aspects of prehistoric life, such as decision-making and social dynamics.

3.4.6 The Legacy of Female Hunters

The discovery of women's participation in group hunts has significant implications for our understanding of prehistoric gender roles. It challenges the long-held assumption that men were the primary hunters and women were confined to gathering activities. This newfound knowledge highlights the complexity and diversity of prehistoric societies, emphasizing the need for a more inclusive and nuanced understanding of gender roles in the past. By recognizing the legacy of female hunters, we can reshape our understanding of human history and promote gender equality in the present.

3.4.7 Future Research and Implications

The revelation of women's role in group hunts opens up new avenues for research and exploration. Further archaeological excavations, anthropological studies, and interdisciplinary collaborations are needed to deepen our understanding of the extent and significance of women's participation in hunting activities. This research can shed light on the social, cultural, and ecological dynamics of prehistoric societies and contribute to a more comprehensive understanding of our ancient ancestors.

In conclusion, the role of women in group hunts was far more significant than previously assumed. Women actively participated in hunting activities, displaying remarkable skills and contributing to the survival and well-being of their communities. Their involvement challenged traditional gender roles and fostered a more egalitarian society. Recognizing the contributions of female hunters not only reshapes our understanding of prehistoric gender roles but also has implications for promoting gender equality in the present.

4

Chapter 4

The Social Dynamics of Hunting

4.1 Hunting as a Cooperative Endeavor

Hunting, as an essential activity for early humans, was not solely the domain of men. Recent research and archaeological evidence have shed light on the cooperative nature of hunting, challenging the traditional assumption that men were the sole hunters while women remained in the cave as gatherers. This chapter explores the cooperative dynamics of hunting and the significant role that women played in this endeavor.

4.1.1 The Power of Cooperation

Hunting, in prehistoric times, was a cooperative endeavor that required the coordination and collaboration of individuals within a group. The success of a hunt depended on the collective efforts of both men and women, each contributing their unique skills and knowledge. This cooperative nature of hunting fostered a sense of unity and interdependence within early human societies.

4.1.2 Women as Skilled Hunters

Contrary to traditional beliefs, women were not passive participants in the hunting process. Archaeological evidence has revealed the presence of female hunters through the discovery of hunting tools and weapons associated with women. These findings challenge the notion that women were solely responsible for gathering activities and highlight their active involvement in hunting.

4.1.3 Division of Labor

The division of labor within hunting groups was not strictly based on gender. Instead, it was determined by individual abilities, strengths, and knowledge. While men may have been physically stronger, women possessed their own unique skills and expertise that contributed to the success of the hunt. This division of labor based on individual capabilities ensured the efficient utilization of resources and increased the chances of survival for the entire group.

4.1.4 Communication and Coordination

Successful hunting required effective communication and coordination among group members. Women played a crucial role in these aspects, utilizing their skills in observation, tracking, and communication to strategize and plan hunts. Their ability to read and interpret environmental cues, such as animal behavior and migration patterns, was invaluable in ensuring the group's success in capturing prey.

4.1.5 Sharing Knowledge and Skills

Hunting was not only a means of survival but also a way to transmit knowledge and skills from one generation to another. Women, as experienced hunters, played a vital role in passing down their hunting techniques, strategies, and knowledge to younger members of the group. This intergenerational transfer of knowledge ensured the continuity and improvement of hunting practices over time.

4.1.6 The Role of Women in Group Dynamics

The active participation of women in hunting had a profound impact on the social dynamics within early human societies. The recognition of women as skilled hunters challenged traditional gender roles and fostered a more egalitarian society. The cooperation and mutual respect between men and women in hunting groups created a sense of equality and contributed to the overall well-being and success of the community.

4.1.7 The Evolution of Cooperation

The cooperative nature of hunting played a significant role in the evolution of early humans. The ability to work together, communicate effectively, and share resources and knowledge enhanced the survival and adaptability of our ancestors. The egalitarian nature of hunting groups, where both men and women actively participated, contributed to the development of complex social structures and the advancement of our species.

4.1.8 The Legacy of Cooperative Hunting

Recognizing the cooperative nature of hunting and the active role of women challenges long-held assumptions about prehistoric gender roles. This new understanding highlights the importance of cooperation, equality, and the value of diverse contributions within a society. By acknowledging the significant role of women as hunters, we gain a more inclusive and accurate understanding of our ancient ancestors and their remarkable achievements.

In the next chapter, we will delve deeper into the gender roles within hunting groups, exploring the dynamics of leadership and decision-making in hunting and the impact of female hunters on group dynamics.

4.2 Gender Roles within Hunting Groups

The exploration of prehistoric gender roles has traditionally depicted men as hunters and women as gatherers, perpetuating the notion that women played a passive role in early human societies. However, recent research and archaeological findings have challenged this conventional narrative, shedding light on the active participation of women as hunters and the complex dynamics within hunting groups. This section delves into the gender roles within hunting groups, highlighting the significant contributions of women and the implications for our understanding of prehistoric societies.

4.2.1 Women as Skilled Hunters

Contrary to popular belief, evidence from various archaeological sites around the world suggests that women were skilled hunters in prehistoric societies. The discovery of female burial sites with hunting tools and weapons, such as spears and projectile points, indicates their active involvement in hunting activities. Additionally, the analysis of skeletal remains has revealed signs of physical stress and injuries consistent with hunting practices in both men and women, further supporting the idea of gender equality in hunting roles.

4.2.2 Cooperative Hunting Strategies

Hunting in prehistoric societies was often a cooperative endeavor, requiring coordination and teamwork within hunting groups. Women played a crucial role in these groups, contributing their skills and knowledge to ensure the success of the hunt. Ethnographic studies of contemporary hunter-gatherer societies provide valuable insights into the division of labor within hunting groups, where women actively participate in hunting alongside men. This suggests that the cooperative nature of hunting was not limited to a specific time period but has been a longstanding practice throughout human history.

4.2.3 Leadership and Decision-Making

The presence of women as hunters challenges the assumption that leadership and decision-making within hunting groups were exclusively male domains. Ethnographic studies of modern hunter-gatherer societies reveal that women often hold positions of authority and influence in hunting activities. They contribute to decision-making processes, such as selecting hunting strategies, identifying prey, and determining the timing and location of hunts. These findings suggest that prehistoric hunting groups may have operated under similar egalitarian principles, with women actively participating in leadership roles.

4.2.4 Gender Dynamics and Social Cohesion

The inclusion of women as hunters in prehistoric societies had profound implications for the social dynamics and cohesion within hunting groups. The active participation of women in hunting fostered a sense of equality and mutual respect among group members. This egalitarian ethos likely contributed to the overall success and survival of the group, as it promoted cooperation, communication, and the sharing of resources. The recognition of women as skilled hunters challenges the notion of a strict gender divide and highlights the importance of a more inclusive understanding of prehistoric gender roles.

4.2.5 The Role of Women in Skill Transmission

The involvement of women as hunters also had implications for the transmission of hunting skills and knowledge within prehistoric societies. Women played a vital role in passing down hunting techniques, strategies, and cultural traditions to future generations. This intergenerational transmission of knowledge ensured the continuity and adaptation of hunting practices over time. By recognizing the active role of women in skill transmission, we gain a deeper appreciation for the complexity and diversity of prehistoric societies.

4.2.6 Challenges and Future Directions

While the evidence supporting the active participation of women as hunters in prehistoric societies is compelling, there are still challenges and gaps in our understanding. The scarcity of archaeological remains and the biases inherent in interpreting past societies pose obstacles to fully reconstructing the lives of ancient huntresses. Future research should employ interdisciplinary approaches, combining archaeological, anthropological, and genetic analyses, to further explore the complexities of gender roles within hunting groups.

In conclusion, the traditional portrayal of prehistoric gender roles as strictly divided between male hunters and female gatherers is being challenged by new research and evidence. The active participation of women as hunters in prehistoric societies highlights the egalitarian nature of early human communities and the importance of recognizing the diverse roles played by both men and women. By embracing a more inclusive understanding of prehistoric gender roles, we gain valuable insights into the complexity and richness of our ancient ancestors' lives.

4.3 Leadership and Decision-Making in Hunting

Leadership and decision-making in hunting played a crucial role in the success of prehistoric hunting groups. While traditional assumptions have often depicted men as the sole leaders in hunting activities, recent research challenges this notion and highlights the significant role that women played in leadership positions within these groups. This section will explore the evidence and theories surrounding leadership and decision-making in hunting, shedding light on the complex dynamics of prehistoric societies.

4.3.1 Leadership Structures in Prehistoric Hunting Groups

The hierarchical structure of prehistoric hunting groups is a topic of ongoing debate among researchers. While some argue that these groups were egalitarian in nature, others propose the existence of leadership roles. Evidence from various archaeological sites suggests that leadership positions were not solely occupied by men but were also held by women.

One line of evidence comes from the analysis of burial sites. In some cases, individuals buried with hunting tools and weapons, traditionally associated with male roles, have been found to be women. This suggests that women held positions of authority and leadership within hunting groups. Additionally, the presence of grave goods associated with hunting, such as animal remains or hunting-related artifacts, further supports the idea of women as leaders in hunting activities.

4.3.2 Decision-Making Processes in Hunting

Effective decision-making was crucial for the success of hunting expeditions. Research indicates that decision-making within prehistoric hunting groups was a collective process, involving both men and women. The decision-making process was likely influenced by various factors, including environmental conditions, available resources, and the expertise of individuals within the group.

Studies of modern-day hunter-gatherer societies provide valuable insights into the decision-making processes of our ancient ancestors. These societies often rely on consensus-based decision-making, where all members of the group have a say in the final decision. This suggests that prehistoric hunting groups may have employed similar decision-making strategies, with both men and women contributing their knowledge and expertise.

4.3.3 Leadership Styles and Strategies

The leadership styles and strategies employed by prehistoric hunting groups likely varied depending on the specific cultural and environmental contexts. Some researchers propose that leadership in hunting groups was based on meritocracy, where individuals with the most skill and knowledge in hunting assumed leadership roles. Others suggest that leadership may have been based on age or experience.

The role of women in leadership positions may have been influenced by their unique skills and abilities. For example, women's knowledge of plant resources and their ability to track and interpret animal behavior may have contributed to their leadership roles in hunting groups. Additionally, women's reproductive capabilities and their role in ensuring the survival of the group may have also played a significant role in their leadership status.

4.3.4 The Impact of Female Leaders on Group Dynamics

The presence of female leaders in prehistoric hunting groups likely had a profound impact on group dynamics. The inclusion of women in leadership positions may have fostered a more egalitarian and cooperative environment within the group. Women's perspectives and decision-making strategies may have complemented those of men, leading to more effective hunting strategies and increased group cohesion.

Furthermore, the presence of female leaders may have challenged traditional gender roles and contributed to a more inclusive and equitable society. The recognition of women as capable leaders in hunting may have influenced other aspects of prehistoric life, such as resource allocation, social organization, and the division of labor.

4.3.5 Challenges and Future Directions

Studying leadership and decision-making in prehistoric hunting groups presents several challenges. The scarcity of direct archaeological evidence and the biases inherent in interpreting past societies make it difficult to reconstruct the exact dynamics of these groups. However, advancements in archaeological techniques and interdisciplinary approaches offer promising avenues for future research.

Future studies could focus on the analysis of ancient artifacts, such as cave paintings and engravings, to gain further insights into the roles and responsibilities of leaders in hunting groups. Additionally, the integration of ethnographic and ethnohistorical data from modern-day hunter-gatherer societies can provide valuable comparative perspectives on leadership and decision-making.

Understanding the leadership and decision-making dynamics in prehistoric hunting groups is crucial for developing a more comprehensive understanding of our ancient ancestors' social structures. By challenging traditional assumptions and recognizing the significant role of women in leadership positions, we can gain a deeper appreciation for the complexity and diversity of prehistoric societies.

4.4 The Impact of Female Hunters on Group Dynamics

The discovery and recognition of female hunters in prehistoric societies have had a profound impact on our understanding of group dynamics during ancient times. This newfound understanding challenges traditional assumptions about gender roles and reveals a more complex and egalitarian social structure among early humans. The inclusion of women as active participants in hunting activities has reshaped our perception of ancient societies and sheds light on the diverse roles and contributions of both men and women.

4.4.1 Redefining Gender Roles within Hunting Groups

The presence of female hunters in prehistoric societies challenges the notion that hunting was exclusively a male domain. It highlights the fact that gender roles were not fixed or rigidly defined, but rather adaptable and dependent on the needs and circumstances of the group. The inclusion of women as hunters suggests a more egalitarian division of labor, where individuals were assigned tasks based on their abilities rather than their gender.

This redefinition of gender roles within hunting groups has significant implications for our understanding of ancient societies. It suggests that women played an active and vital role in securing food resources for their communities, contributing to the survival and well-being of the group as a whole. The recognition of female hunters also challenges the idea that women were solely responsible for gathering activities, emphasizing their agency and autonomy in decision-making processes related to subsistence strategies.

4.4.2 Cooperation and Collaboration in Hunting

The presence of female hunters also highlights the importance of cooperation and collaboration within hunting groups. Hunting was not an individual endeavor but a collective effort that required coordination, communication, and shared knowledge. The inclusion of women as hunters suggests that gender did not determine an individual's ability to contribute effectively to the group's success.

The impact of female hunters on group dynamics can be seen in the increased diversity of skills and perspectives within hunting groups. Women brought their unique experiences and insights to the table, enriching the collective knowledge and enhancing the group's ability to adapt to changing environments and challenges. The inclusion of women as hunters fostered a sense of equality and mutual respect within the group, promoting a more cohesive and harmonious social structure.

4.4.3 Leadership and Decision-Making in Hunting

The recognition of female hunters also challenges traditional assumptions about leadership and decision-making within hunting groups. It suggests that leadership roles were not exclusively reserved for men but were based on individual capabilities and expertise. Women who demonstrated exceptional hunting skills and knowledge could assume leadership positions within their communities, influencing the group's hunting strategies and decision-making processes.

The impact of female hunters on group dynamics can be seen in the diversification of leadership styles and approaches. The inclusion of women as leaders brought a different perspective and leadership style to the table, promoting a more inclusive and collaborative decision-making process. This diversity in leadership enhanced the group's ability to adapt to changing circumstances, ensuring the survival and success of the community.

4.4.4 Social Cohesion and Gender Equality

The recognition of female hunters has significant implications for our understanding of social cohesion and gender equality in prehistoric societies. The inclusion of women as active participants in hunting activities challenges the notion of a strictly patriarchal social structure and highlights the existence of more egalitarian and cooperative relationships between men and women.

The impact of female hunters on group dynamics can be seen in the promotion of gender equality and the dismantling of gender stereotypes. The recognition of women as skilled hunters challenges the idea that certain tasks or roles are inherently gendered, emphasizing the importance of individual capabilities and contributions. This recognition fosters a more inclusive and equitable society, where individuals are valued for their skills and abilities rather than their gender.

The presence of female hunters also promotes social cohesion within the group. The inclusion of women in hunting activities strengthens the bonds between individuals, fostering a sense of shared responsibility and interdependence. This increased social cohesion contributes to the overall well-being and resilience of the community, ensuring its survival and success in challenging environments.

In conclusion, the recognition of female hunters in prehistoric societies has had a transformative impact on our understanding of group dynamics. It challenges traditional assumptions about gender roles, redefines leadership and decision-making processes, and promotes social cohesion and gender equality. The inclusion of women as active participants in hunting activities reveals a more complex and egalitarian social structure among early humans, highlighting the diverse roles and contributions of both men and women. This newfound understanding opens up new avenues for research and encourages a more inclusive and comprehensive understanding of prehistoric gender roles.

5

Chapter 5

Hunting and Survival

5.1 The Importance of Hunting for Early Humans

Hunting played a crucial role in the survival and development of early humans. For millions of years, our ancient ancestors relied on hunting as a means of sustenance, shaping their societies, and driving the evolution of human intelligence. The discovery that women were active hunters challenges traditional assumptions about prehistoric gender roles and provides valuable insights into the complexity of early human societies.

5.1.1 Hunting as a Source of Food

Hunting provided early humans with a reliable source of protein and essential nutrients. In the harsh environments of the prehistoric world, where food scarcity was a constant threat, the ability to hunt and secure meat was vital for survival. The nutritional benefits of hunting, such as high-quality protein and fat, played a significant role in the physical development and overall health of early humans.

5.1.2 Hunting and the Evolution of Human Intelligence

The act of hunting required complex cognitive abilities, including planning, strategizing, and problem-solving. Early humans had to understand the behavior of their prey, anticipate their movements, and devise effective hunting techniques. These cognitive demands stimulated the development of intelligence and problem-solving skills, contributing to the evolution of the human brain.

5.1.3 The Role of Female Hunters in Group Survival

The discovery of female hunters challenges the notion that hunting was exclusively a male activity. In many hunter-gatherer societies, women actively participated in hunting alongside men, contributing to the overall success and survival of the group. The involvement of women in hunting diversified the group's food sources, reduced the burden on male hunters, and increased the overall efficiency of the hunting endeavor.

5.1.4 Hunting and Social Dynamics

Hunting was not merely a means of acquiring food but also a social activity that fostered cooperation and strengthened social bonds within early human communities. Group hunts required coordination, communication, and shared decision-making. The inclusion of women as hunters would have influenced the social dynamics within these groups, challenging traditional gender roles and promoting a more egalitarian society.

5.1.5 Hunting and Cultural Significance

The importance of hunting extended beyond its practical benefits. Hunting held cultural and symbolic significance for early humans, as evidenced by the artistic representations found in cave paintings and petroglyphs. These depictions often portrayed both men and women engaged in hunting activities, highlighting the equal participation of women in this essential aspect of early human life.

5.1.6 The Legacy of Female Hunters

Recognizing the role of female hunters in prehistoric societies has profound implications for our understanding of gender roles and the history of human civilization. It challenges the long-held assumption that men were the sole providers and hunters, while women were confined to domestic tasks. The recognition of female hunters empowers women today by highlighting their historical contributions and challenging gender stereotypes that persist in modern society.

5.1.7 The Importance of Challenging Assumptions

The discovery of female hunters emphasizes the need to challenge assumptions and biases in archaeological research. By questioning traditional gender roles, we gain a more accurate and inclusive understanding of prehistoric societies. This shift in perspective encourages further exploration and research into the lives of our ancient ancestors, shedding light on the complexity and diversity of early human societies.

5.1.8 Implications for Modern Gender Equality

The recognition of female hunters in prehistoric societies has implications for modern gender equality. It challenges the notion that gender roles are fixed and highlights the potential for gender equality in all aspects of life. By acknowledging the historical contributions of women as hunters, we can promote a more inclusive and equitable society, where individuals are not limited by societal expectations based on gender.

In conclusion, hunting played a vital role in the survival and development of early humans. The discovery of female hunters challenges traditional assumptions about prehistoric gender roles and provides valuable insights into the complexity of early human societies. Hunting was not only a means of acquiring food but also a catalyst for the evolution of human intelligence and the development of social dynamics. Recognizing the importance of hunting and the participation of women as hunters in prehistoric societies has profound implications for our understanding of gender roles and the promotion of gender equality in modern society.

5.2 Nutritional Benefits of Hunting

Hunting played a crucial role in the survival and development of early human societies. It provided not only a source of food but also various nutritional benefits that contributed to the overall health and well-being of our ancient ancestors. In this section, we will explore the nutritional advantages of hunting and how it shaped the evolution of early humans.

5.2.1 A Diverse and Nutrient-Rich Diet

Hunting allowed early humans to access a wide range of animal species, each offering a unique nutritional profile. Unlike a solely plant-based diet, hunting provided a rich source of high-quality protein, essential fatty acids, and micronutrients that were vital for the growth and development of our ancient ancestors. Animal protein is considered a complete protein, containing all the essential amino acids necessary for human health. This ensured that early humans had access to a well-rounded and balanced diet, promoting optimal physical and cognitive development.

5.2.2 Increased Energy Intake

The act of hunting itself required significant physical exertion, which resulted in increased energy expenditure. To compensate for this, early humans needed to consume a higher number of calories to sustain their energy levels. Hunting provided an opportunity to acquire calorie-dense foods, such as meat and animal fat, which supplied the necessary energy for survival. This increased energy intake from hunting allowed early humans to engage in other physically demanding activities, such as tool-making, social interactions, and exploration, further contributing to their overall well-being.

5.2.3 Essential Nutrients for Brain Development

The nutritional benefits of hunting extended beyond physical health and played a crucial role in the development of the human brain. Animal-based foods, particularly those rich in omega-3 fatty acids, provided essential nutrients that supported brain growth and function. Omega-3 fatty acids, found abundantly in fish and other marine animals, are known to enhance cognitive abilities, improve memory, and promote overall brain health. The consumption of these nutrient-dense foods through hunting likely played a significant role in the evolution of human intelligence.

5.2.4 Micronutrients and Health Benefits

Hunting also provided early humans with access to a variety of micronutrients that were essential for maintaining good health. Animal-based foods are rich in vitamins, minerals, and trace elements that are crucial for various bodily functions. For example, iron from red meat is essential for oxygen transport in the body, while vitamin B12, primarily found in animal products, is necessary for the production of red blood cells and the proper functioning of the nervous system. By incorporating a diverse range of animal species into their diet through hunting, early humans ensured that they received an adequate supply of these vital micronutrients.

5.2.5 Adaptation to Changing Environments

The ability to hunt and consume animal-based foods also provided early humans with a significant advantage in adapting to different environments. Unlike plants, which are often limited to specific regions and seasons, animals can be found in various habitats and climates. This flexibility allowed early humans to explore and settle in diverse environments, expanding their range and increasing their chances of survival. The nutritional benefits of hunting played a crucial role in enabling our ancient ancestors to thrive in different ecosystems and adapt to changing environmental conditions.

5.2.6 The Role of Female Hunters in Nutritional Provisioning

The recognition of female hunters challenges the traditional assumption that hunting was solely a male activity. The involvement of women in hunting expeditions would have had a profound impact on the nutritional well-being of early human communities. By actively participating in hunting, women would have contributed to the acquisition of a diverse range of animal-based foods, enriching the overall nutritional profile of the group's diet. This would have had significant implications for the health and development of both women and their offspring, further emphasizing the importance of female hunters in ensuring the survival and success of early human societies.

In conclusion, hunting provided early humans with numerous nutritional benefits that were crucial for their survival and development. The consumption of animal-based foods through hunting ensured a diverse and nutrient-rich diet, promoting optimal physical and cognitive growth. The recognition of female hunters challenges traditional gender roles and highlights the significant contributions women made to the nutritional provisioning of early human communities. Understanding the nutritional benefits of hunting provides valuable insights into the lives of our ancient ancestors and the factors that shaped our evolutionary journey.

5.3 Hunting and the Evolution of Human Intelligence

Hunting played a crucial role in the survival and development of early humans. It not only provided sustenance but also shaped the evolution of human intelligence. The participation of women in hunting activities further contributed to the complexity and adaptability of our species. This section explores the relationship between hunting and the evolution of human intelligence, highlighting the significant role of female hunters in this process.

5.3.1 The Cognitive Demands of Hunting

Hunting required early humans to develop a range of cognitive skills, including problem-solving, planning, and cooperation. Tracking and capturing prey demanded keen observation, strategic thinking, and the ability to anticipate the movements and behavior of animals. These cognitive demands stimulated the development of the human brain, leading to the evolution of higher intelligence.

5.3.2 The Role of Female Hunters in Cognitive Development

Contrary to traditional assumptions, recent research has revealed that women were active participants in hunting activities. This challenges the notion that hunting was exclusively a male domain. The involvement of women in hunting expeditions would have provided them with opportunities to develop the same cognitive skills as their male counterparts. This shared participation in hunting activities would have contributed to the overall cognitive development of early human communities.

5.3.3 Cooperative Hunting and Social Intelligence

Hunting was often a cooperative endeavor, requiring individuals to work together to successfully capture prey. This cooperative nature of hunting fostered the development of social intelligence, as individuals had to communicate, coordinate, and share knowledge and resources. The inclusion of women in hunting groups would have enhanced the diversity of skills and perspectives, further enriching the social dynamics and collective intelligence of early human communities.

5.3.4 The Evolutionary Advantage of Female Hunters

The participation of women in hunting activities provided several evolutionary advantages. Firstly, it diversified the food sources available to the community, reducing the risk of food scarcity and increasing overall survival rates. Secondly, it allowed for the sharing of physical exertion and risk, ensuring the well-being of both men and women. This division of labor based on individual strengths and abilities would have increased the overall efficiency and success of hunting expeditions.

5.3.5 The Cognitive Benefits of Hunting for Women

Engaging in hunting activities would have provided women with unique cognitive benefits. The challenges and complexities of hunting would have stimulated their cognitive abilities, enhancing their problem-solving skills, spatial awareness, and adaptability. These cognitive benefits would have extended beyond the hunting context, positively influencing other aspects of their lives and contributing to the overall cognitive development of early human communities.

5.3.6 The Impact of Female Hunters on Cultural Evolution

The inclusion of women as hunters would have had profound implications for the cultural evolution of early human societies. The sharing of hunting knowledge and skills between men and women would have facilitated the transmission of cultural practices and the accumulation of collective knowledge. This exchange of information would have contributed to the development of more sophisticated hunting techniques and tools, further enhancing the adaptability and survival of early human communities.

5.3.7 The Legacy of Female Hunters in Human Society

Recognizing the role of female hunters in the evolution of human intelligence challenges traditional gender stereotypes and provides a more inclusive understanding of prehistoric gender roles. It highlights the importance of gender equality and the contributions of women throughout human history. Understanding the legacy of female hunters can empower women in contemporary society, inspiring them to pursue their passions and challenge societal expectations.

5.3.8 Future Research Directions

While recent research has shed light on the participation of women in hunting activities, there is still much to uncover. Future research should explore the specific roles and responsibilities of female hunters in different cultural contexts and environments. Additionally, advancements in archaeological techniques and technologies can provide further insights into the cognitive development and social dynamics of early human communities.

In conclusion, hunting played a pivotal role in the evolution of human intelligence. The participation of women as hunters challenged traditional gender roles and contributed to the cognitive development and cultural evolution of early human communities. Recognizing the significance of female hunters provides a more comprehensive understanding of our ancient ancestors and emphasizes the importance of gender equality in both the past and present.

5.4 The Role of Female Hunters in Ensuring Group Survival

Throughout history, the prevailing narrative has often depicted men as the primary hunters and women as gatherers, playing a secondary role in the survival of early human groups. However, recent research and archaeological findings have challenged this assumption, shedding light on the significant role of female hunters in ensuring the survival of their communities. This chapter explores the vital contributions of female hunters and their impact on group dynamics and overall group survival.

5.4.1 The Evolution of Cooperative Hunting

Cooperative hunting played a crucial role in the survival of early human groups, and women were active participants in this endeavor. Research suggests that hunting was a collaborative effort, with both men and women working together to secure food resources for their communities. The division of labor was not strictly based on gender, but rather on individual skills and abilities.

5.4.2 The Adaptive Advantage of Female Hunters

The inclusion of female hunters in early human societies provided several adaptive advantages. Women's participation in hunting diversified the food sources available to the group, reducing the risk of food scarcity and increasing overall resilience. Additionally, female hunters contributed to the social cohesion of the group, fostering cooperation and strengthening interpersonal relationships.

5.4.3 Hunting Strategies and Techniques

Female hunters employed a variety of strategies and techniques to secure food for their communities. While the specific methods varied depending on the environment and available resources, women developed their own hunting skills and utilized a range of tools and weapons. Archaeological evidence has revealed the presence of female-specific hunting implements, indicating their active involvement in the hunting process.

5.4.4 The Role of Female Hunters in Group Dynamics

The participation of women in hunting had a profound impact on the social dynamics of early human groups. Female hunters challenged traditional gender roles and contributed to a more egalitarian society. Their involvement in hunting fostered a sense of equality and mutual respect within the group, as individuals were valued for their skills and contributions rather than their gender.

5.4.5 The Importance of Female Hunters in Childrearing

Contrary to the notion that women solely focused on childrearing and domestic tasks, female hunters played a vital role in ensuring the survival and well-being of their offspring. By actively participating in hunting, women provided their children with a consistent and reliable food source, contributing to their overall health and development. This active involvement in the food procurement process also allowed women to pass on valuable knowledge and skills to future generations.

5.4.6 The Impact of Female Hunters on Group Survival

The inclusion of female hunters significantly enhanced the survival prospects of early human groups. By diversifying food sources and contributing to the overall food security of the community, women played a crucial role in mitigating the risks associated with food scarcity. The active participation of women in hunting also increased the overall efficiency and success rate of hunting expeditions, ensuring a steady supply of food for the group.

5.4.7 The Legacy of Female Hunters

The recognition of female hunters in prehistoric societies challenges long-held assumptions about gender roles and highlights the importance of a more inclusive understanding of our ancient ancestors. By acknowledging the significant contributions of women in hunting and group survival, we gain a deeper appreciation for the complexity and diversity of early human societies. This recognition also has implications for modern gender equality, as it challenges the notion that certain roles are inherently gendered.

5.4.8 Future Directions in Research

While recent research has shed light on the role of female hunters, there are still many unanswered questions and avenues for future exploration. Further archaeological excavations, interdisciplinary collaborations, and advancements in analytical techniques hold the potential to uncover additional evidence and provide a more comprehensive understanding of the lives of ancient female hunters. By continuing to challenge assumptions and biases, we can continue to expand our knowledge and appreciation of prehistoric gender roles.

In conclusion, the role of female hunters in ensuring group survival cannot be understated. Their active participation in hunting expeditions, their contributions to food security, and their impact on group dynamics all played a vital role in the survival and success of early human communities. Recognizing the importance of female hunters challenges traditional gender roles and provides a more accurate and inclusive understanding of our ancient ancestors. By embracing this new perspective, we can gain valuable insights into the complexity and diversity of prehistoric societies and pave the way for a more equitable future.

6

Chapter 6

Artistic Representations of Female Hunters

6.1 Cave Paintings and Petroglyphs

Cave paintings and petroglyphs provide a fascinating glimpse into the lives of our ancient ancestors. These artistic representations, created thousands of years ago, offer valuable insights into the activities, beliefs, and social dynamics of prehistoric societies. In the context of our exploration of prehistoric gender roles, cave paintings and petroglyphs play a crucial role in shedding light on the participation of women in hunting activities.

6.1.1 Depictions of Female Hunters

One of the most striking aspects of cave paintings and petroglyphs is the presence of female figures engaged in hunting scenes. These depictions challenge the traditional notion that hunting was exclusively a male activity. Instead, they suggest that women played an active role in hunting and were integral members of hunting groups.

In many cave paintings, we see female figures depicted alongside male figures, both armed with weapons and engaged in hunting activities. These representations indicate that women were not merely passive observers or gatherers but actively participated in the hunt. The presence of women in these scenes suggests a level of gender equality and cooperation that is often overlooked in our understanding of prehistoric societies.

6.1.2 Symbolism and Meaning in Ancient Art

Cave paintings and petroglyphs not only depict the physical act of hunting but also convey symbolic and cultural meanings. These artistic representations provide valuable insights into the beliefs, rituals, and social structures of prehistoric communities.

The inclusion of female hunters in these artworks suggests that women held a significant role in the cultural and spiritual life of these societies. The symbolism associated with female hunters may have represented concepts such as fertility, strength, and the ability to provide for the community. These depictions challenge the notion that women were solely responsible for gathering and nurturing, highlighting their active participation in the survival and well-being of the group.

6.1.3 Depictions of Female Hunters in Mythology and Folklore

Beyond cave paintings and petroglyphs, the presence of female hunters can also be found in the mythology and folklore of various ancient cultures. These stories and legends further reinforce the idea that women played a vital role in hunting activities.

For example, in certain Native American tribes, there are myths and legends that depict powerful female hunters who possessed exceptional skills and knowledge of the natural world. These stories not only celebrate the prowess of female hunters but also emphasize their importance in the cultural and spiritual fabric of the community.

6.1.4 The Legacy of Female Hunters in Artistic Traditions

The recognition of female hunters in cave paintings and petroglyphs has had a profound impact on artistic traditions throughout history. Artists, inspired by these ancient depictions, have continued to portray women as hunters in various forms of art.

From classical paintings to contemporary sculptures, the legacy of female hunters can be seen in the artistic representations of women engaged in hunting activities. These artworks challenge traditional gender roles and celebrate the strength, skill, and resilience of women as hunters.

The inclusion of female hunters in artistic traditions not only serves as a reminder of our ancient past but also challenges societal norms and expectations. It encourages us to question and reevaluate our assumptions about gender roles, both in the past and in the present.

In conclusion, cave paintings and petroglyphs provide valuable evidence of the active participation of women in hunting activities during prehistoric times. These artistic representations challenge the conventional portrayal of prehistoric gender roles and highlight the importance of recognizing the egalitarian nature of our ancient ancestors. The depictions of female hunters in cave paintings and petroglyphs, along with their presence in mythology and folklore, emphasize the significant role women played in hunting and the broader social dynamics of prehistoric societies. The legacy of female hunters in artistic traditions further reinforces the importance of challenging gender stereotypes and embracing a more inclusive understanding of prehistoric gender roles.

6.2 Symbolism and Meaning in Ancient Art

Art has always been a powerful medium for expressing ideas, beliefs, and cultural values. In the context of prehistoric societies, artistic representations provide valuable insights into the symbolism and meaning associated with various aspects of life, including the roles and activities of individuals within the community. This chapter explores the artistic representations of female hunters in ancient art and delves into the symbolism and meaning behind these depictions.

6.2.1 Artistic Representations of Female Hunters

The artistic representations of female hunters in prehistoric art offer a fascinating glimpse into the lives and activities of ancient women. These depictions can be found in various forms, such as cave paintings, petroglyphs, and sculptures. While the exact interpretation of these artworks may vary, they collectively contribute to our understanding of the significance of female hunting in prehistoric societies.

Cave paintings, dating back thousands of years, often depict scenes of hunting expeditions. These paintings provide vivid illustrations of the hunting techniques, tools, and the participation of both men and women in these activities. Interestingly, some cave paintings specifically highlight the presence of female hunters, challenging the traditional notion that hunting was exclusively a male domain.

Petroglyphs, carved into rock surfaces, also offer valuable insights into the representation of female hunters. These engravings often depict women engaged in hunting activities, using various weapons and tools. The presence of these depictions suggests that female hunting was not only a practical reality but also held cultural and symbolic significance within these ancient societies.

6.2.2 Symbolism and Meaning in Ancient Art

The symbolism and meaning associated with the artistic representations of female hunters in ancient art are multifaceted. These depictions not only reflect the practical aspects of hunting but also convey deeper cultural and social messages.

One interpretation of these artworks suggests that the portrayal of female hunters symbolizes the importance and value placed on women's contributions to the survival and well-being of the community. By depicting women engaged in hunting, these artworks challenge the notion that women were solely responsible for gathering and domestic tasks. They highlight the active participation of women in activities traditionally associated with men, emphasizing the egalitarian nature of prehistoric societies.

Furthermore, the artistic representations of female hunters may also signify the spiritual and symbolic connection between women and the natural world. Hunting, as a means of procuring food and resources, was deeply intertwined with the cycles of nature. By depicting women as hunters, these artworks may symbolize the harmonious relationship between women, nature, and the sustenance of the community.

6.2.3 Depictions of Female Hunters in Mythology and Folklore

In addition to cave paintings and petroglyphs, depictions of female hunters can also be found in the mythology and folklore of various ancient cultures. These narratives further reinforce the significance of female hunting and its cultural and symbolic implications.

Mythological stories often feature powerful female figures who possess exceptional hunting skills and prowess. These female hunters are portrayed as strong, independent, and capable individuals who play crucial roles in the survival and prosperity of their communities. Their stories serve as inspiration and affirmation of the capabilities and contributions of women in prehistoric societies.

Folklore, passed down through generations, also contains tales of female hunters. These stories not only entertain but also serve as a means of preserving cultural knowledge and values. By including female hunters in these narratives, ancient societies acknowledged and celebrated the important role of women in hunting and the wider community.

6.2.4 The Legacy of Female Hunters in Artistic Traditions

The artistic representations of female hunters in prehistoric art have left a lasting legacy in artistic traditions throughout history. These depictions have influenced subsequent artistic movements, challenging gender norms and inspiring new interpretations of femininity and strength.

In later periods, such as ancient Greece and Rome, female hunters continued to be depicted in various art forms, including pottery, sculptures, and mosaics. These representations often portrayed women engaged in hunting activities, highlighting their physical prowess and skill. The enduring presence of female hunters in artistic traditions underscores the enduring impact of prehistoric gender roles on subsequent societies.

Furthermore, the recognition of female hunters in prehistoric art has also influenced contemporary artists. Many modern artists draw inspiration from these ancient depictions, using them as a means to challenge gender stereotypes and explore the complexities of gender identity and roles in society.

Conclusion

The artistic representations of female hunters in prehistoric art provide valuable insights into the symbolism and meaning associated with the roles of women in ancient societies. These depictions challenge traditional assumptions about prehistoric gender roles and highlight the active participation of women in hunting activities. The symbolism and meaning behind these artworks reflect the cultural and social significance of female hunting, emphasizing the egalitarian nature of prehistoric communities. The legacy of female hunters in artistic traditions throughout history continues to inspire and challenge contemporary interpretations of gender roles and identities. By recognizing and understanding the symbolism and meaning in ancient art, we gain a deeper appreciation for the diverse and complex lives of our ancient huntresses.

6.3 Depictions of Female Hunters in Mythology and Folklore

Throughout history, mythology and folklore have served as powerful mediums for expressing cultural beliefs, values, and societal norms. These narratives often reflect the collective imagination and experiences of a society, offering insights into the roles and identities of different individuals within that culture. In the case of prehistoric gender roles, mythology and folklore provide us with a fascinating glimpse into the depiction of female hunters and their significance in ancient societies.

6.3.1 Goddesses of the Hunt

One of the most prominent depictions of female hunters in mythology can be found in the figure of the huntress goddess. Across various ancient cultures, goddesses associated with hunting and the wilderness were revered and celebrated. These goddesses embodied the qualities of strength, agility, and skill that were essential for successful hunting. They were often depicted with bows, arrows, and other hunting tools, symbolizing their prowess in the hunt.

In Greek mythology, Artemis, the goddess of the hunt, was a central figure. She was known for her independence, fierce determination, and her ability to protect and provide for herself. Artemis was often portrayed as a skilled huntress, accompanied by a group of nymphs who shared in her hunting activities. Her depiction as a powerful and capable hunter challenged traditional gender roles and highlighted the importance of female hunters in ancient societies.

Similarly, in Norse mythology, the goddess Skadi was associated with hunting, skiing, and archery. Skadi was known for her exceptional hunting skills and her ability to survive in the harsh wilderness. Her portrayal as a skilled huntress emphasized the significance of women in hunting and their ability to contribute to the survival and well-being of their communities.

6.3.2 Folklore and Heroic Tales

In addition to mythology, folklore and heroic tales from different cultures also provide glimpses of female hunters. These stories often feature strong and courageous women who embark on hunting expeditions, showcasing their skills and bravery. These narratives challenge the notion that hunting was solely a male domain and highlight the active participation of women in hunting activities.

For example, in Native American folklore, there are numerous stories of female hunters who possess exceptional hunting abilities. These women are often portrayed as skilled markswomen and trackers, capable of providing food and resources for their communities. These tales not only celebrate the hunting prowess of women but also emphasize their integral role in the survival and well-being of their tribes.

Similarly, in African folklore, there are stories of female hunters who navigate the wilderness with ease and precision. These women are depicted as knowledgeable about the habits and behaviors of animals, enabling them to successfully hunt and provide for their families. These tales challenge the notion that hunting was exclusively a male endeavor and highlight the importance of female hunters in traditional African societies.

6.3.3 Symbolism and Empowerment

The depiction of female hunters in mythology and folklore goes beyond mere representation. These narratives often carry symbolic meanings and serve as sources of empowerment for women. By portraying women as skilled hunters, these stories challenge societal norms and expectations, encouraging women to embrace their own strength, independence, and capabilities.

The symbolism associated with female hunters in mythology and folklore also extends to the broader understanding of gender roles and equality. These depictions challenge the notion that certain activities or roles are inherently gendered, emphasizing the importance of recognizing and valuing the diverse contributions of individuals within a society.

6.3.4 Cultural Significance and Legacy

The depictions of female hunters in mythology and folklore have had a lasting impact on cultural beliefs and traditions. These narratives have shaped the perception of women's roles and abilities, challenging the notion of women as passive gatherers and highlighting their active participation in hunting activities.

Furthermore, the recognition of female hunters in mythology and folklore has the potential to reshape our understanding of prehistoric gender roles. By acknowledging the existence and significance of female hunters in ancient societies, we can challenge the long-held assumptions that have perpetuated gender inequalities and limited our understanding of the past.

The depictions of female hunters in mythology and folklore serve as a reminder of the rich and diverse history of human societies. They provide evidence of the egalitarian nature of early human communities and the active participation of women in hunting activities. By exploring these narratives, we can gain a deeper appreciation for the contributions of female hunters and their impact on the social dynamics and survival of ancient societies.

As we continue to uncover more evidence and challenge traditional assumptions, it is crucial to recognize the importance of mythology and folklore in shaping our understanding of prehistoric gender roles. These narratives offer valuable insights into the lives and experiences of our ancient huntresses, reminding us of the complex and multifaceted nature of human history.

6.4 The Legacy of Female Hunters in Artistic Traditions

Artistic traditions have long served as a window into the beliefs, values, and daily lives of ancient civilizations. In the case of prehistoric societies, artistic representations provide invaluable insights into the roles and activities of individuals within these communities. The legacy of female hunters in artistic traditions is a testament to the significant contributions and presence of women in prehistoric hunting societies.

6.4.1 Cave Paintings and Petroglyphs

One of the most remarkable forms of artistic representation from prehistoric times is cave paintings and petroglyphs. These ancient artworks, found in various parts of the world, offer glimpses into the lives of our ancestors and their interactions with the natural world. Among the diverse range of subjects depicted in these artworks, the presence of female hunters is a recurring theme.

In many cave paintings, we see vivid depictions of women engaged in hunting activities. These images often portray women armed with weapons, such as spears or bows, actively participating in the pursuit of game. The attention to detail and the skillful execution of these artworks suggest that female hunters held a significant place within their communities.

6.4.2 Symbolism and Meaning in Ancient Art

The artistic representations of female hunters in prehistoric art carry profound symbolism and meaning. These depictions not only reflect the reality of women's involvement in hunting but also convey deeper cultural and social messages. The presence of female hunters in art challenges the notion of gender roles and highlights the egalitarian nature of prehistoric societies.

In some instances, the portrayal of female hunters in art may symbolize fertility and the life-giving power of women. The act of hunting, traditionally associated with strength and prowess, becomes a metaphor for the nurturing and protective qualities of women. These artistic representations serve as a testament to the multifaceted roles women played in prehistoric communities.

6.4.3 Depictions of Female Hunters in Mythology and Folklore

Beyond cave paintings and petroglyphs, the legacy of female hunters is also evident in the mythology and folklore of various ancient cultures. Stories and legends passed down through generations often feature powerful female figures engaged in hunting activities. These narratives not only celebrate the skills and bravery of female hunters but also reinforce the idea of gender equality within these societies.

In many mythological tales, female hunters are depicted as heroines, revered for their hunting prowess and revered for their ability to provide for their communities. These stories challenge the notion that hunting was solely a male domain and emphasize the importance of women's contributions to the survival and well-being of their groups.

6.4.4 The Evolution of Artistic Representations

The artistic representations of female hunters have evolved over time, reflecting the changing cultural and societal dynamics. As societies transitioned from hunter-gatherer to agrarian lifestyles, the prominence of female hunters in art gradually diminished. The shift towards a more sedentary lifestyle and the emergence of gendered divisions of labor influenced the portrayal of women in artistic traditions.

However, even in later artistic traditions, glimpses of the legacy of female hunters can still be found. In some ancient civilizations, such as the Scythians or the Amazons, women continued to be depicted as skilled warriors and hunters. These representations serve as a reminder of the enduring legacy of female hunters and challenge the notion that women's involvement in hunting was a fleeting phenomenon.

6.4.5 Inspiring Modern Art and Interpretations

The legacy of female hunters in artistic traditions continues to inspire contemporary artists and researchers. The recognition of women's historical role as hunters has sparked new artistic interpretations and explorations of prehistoric gender dynamics. Artists, through their work, aim to challenge traditional gender stereotypes and shed light on the rich and diverse history of women's contributions to hunting societies.

Furthermore, the artistic representations of female hunters have also influenced the field of archaeology and anthropology. Researchers now approach the study of prehistoric gender roles with a more inclusive lens, acknowledging the significant role women played in hunting and the broader social dynamics of ancient societies.

In conclusion, the legacy of female hunters in artistic traditions is a testament to the important role women played in prehistoric hunting societies. Cave paintings, petroglyphs, mythology, and folklore all provide evidence of women's active participation in hunting activities. These artistic representations challenge traditional gender roles and highlight the egalitarian nature of prehistoric communities. The evolving nature of artistic traditions reflects the changing dynamics of societies over time but does not diminish the significance of women's contributions. The legacy of female hunters continues to inspire modern art and research, fostering a more inclusive understanding of prehistoric gender roles.

7

Chapter 7

Challenging Gender Stereotypes

7.1 The Impact of Gender Stereotypes on Archaeological Interpretations

Gender stereotypes have played a significant role in shaping our understanding of prehistoric societies and their gender roles. For centuries, the prevailing assumption was that men were the primary hunters, while women were confined to gathering activities and domestic tasks. This biased interpretation of prehistoric gender roles has influenced archaeological research and hindered our ability to recognize the true diversity and complexity of ancient societies.

7.1.1 The Influence of Bias

The impact of gender stereotypes on archaeological interpretations cannot be underestimated. These stereotypes have shaped the questions asked, the methods employed, and the conclusions drawn by researchers. The assumption that men were the dominant hunters has led to a focus on studying hunting tools and techniques associated with male activities, while neglecting the potential contributions of women in this domain.

This bias has resulted in a skewed representation of prehistoric societies, perpetuating the notion that women were passive participants in the survival of their communities. By overlooking the role of women as hunters, archaeologists have inadvertently reinforced gender stereotypes and limited our understanding of the past.

7.1.2 Challenging Assumptions

Fortunately, recent archaeological discoveries and a reevaluation of existing evidence have challenged these long-held assumptions. The recognition of female hunters in prehistoric societies has emerged as a groundbreaking revelation, overturning the traditional narrative of gender roles.

Archaeological sites around the world have yielded compelling evidence of female participation in hunting activities. The discovery of ancient burial sites containing female individuals buried with hunting tools and weapons provides tangible proof of their involvement in hunting. Additionally, the analysis of skeletal remains has revealed physical indicators of hunting-related activities in both male and female individuals, further dispelling the notion of gender-specific roles.

7.1.3 Reinterpreting the Evidence

Reevaluating the existing archaeological evidence through a gender-neutral lens is crucial for a more accurate understanding of prehistoric gender roles. By challenging the assumptions and biases that have influenced previous interpretations, researchers can uncover the true extent of female participation in hunting and other activities.

This reevaluation requires a multidisciplinary approach, combining archaeological, anthropological, and paleontological perspectives. By examining a wide range of evidence, including tool assemblages, animal remains, and artistic representations, researchers can piece together a more comprehensive picture of prehistoric societies and the roles played by both men and women.

7.1.4 Uncovering Hidden Narratives

The impact of gender stereotypes on archaeological interpretations extends beyond the realm of gender roles. It also affects our understanding of social dynamics, leadership, and decision-making within prehistoric communities. By recognizing the active participation of women in hunting, we can begin to uncover the hidden narratives of female agency, cooperation, and leadership that have been overlooked for far too long.

Reevaluating prehistoric gender roles not only challenges our understanding of the past but also has profound implications for modern society. It highlights the fallacy of rigid gender stereotypes and emphasizes the importance of equality and inclusivity. By acknowledging the historical existence of female hunters, we can challenge and dismantle the gender biases that persist in contemporary society.

7.1.5 The Need for Further Research

While significant progress has been made in challenging gender stereotypes and reevaluating prehistoric gender roles, there is still much work to be done. The impact of gender stereotypes on archaeological interpretations underscores the need for further research and exploration.

Future studies should focus on filling the gaps in our knowledge, exploring the nuances of gender roles within different prehistoric societies, and investigating the factors that influenced the division of labor. Advancements in archaeological techniques and technologies, such as DNA analysis and isotopic studies, offer promising avenues for uncovering more evidence and shedding light on the lives of our ancient ancestors.

7.1.6 A Call for Inclusivity

Recognizing the impact of gender stereotypes on archaeological interpretations is not only a scholarly endeavor but also a call for inclusivity and equality. By challenging these biases, we can create a more accurate and comprehensive understanding of prehistoric societies, one that reflects the true diversity and complexity of human experiences.

This reevaluation of prehistoric gender roles has the potential to reshape our understanding of gender equality throughout history. It serves as a reminder that gender roles are not fixed or universal but are shaped by cultural, social, and environmental factors. By embracing a more inclusive perspective, we can learn valuable lessons from our ancient huntresses and strive for a more equitable future.

7.2 Reevaluating Prehistoric Gender Roles

The conventional portrayal of prehistoric gender roles as men being hunters and women being gatherers is being challenged by recent findings and research. This new evidence suggests that women were not just gatherers who stayed inside the cave, but active hunters who played a significant role in the survival and success of early human communities. This reevaluation of prehistoric gender roles is not only reshaping our understanding of our ancient ancestors but also highlighting the importance of recognizing the egalitarian nature of early human societies.

7.2.1 The Shift in Paradigm

For many years, the prevailing assumption was that men were the primary hunters while women were responsible for gathering plant-based resources and taking care of domestic tasks. This assumption was largely based on modern gender roles and cultural biases, rather than concrete evidence from the past. However, as archaeological and anthropological research has advanced, a more nuanced and accurate picture of prehistoric gender roles has emerged.

7.2.2 Archaeological Discoveries

Archaeological findings have provided compelling evidence of female hunters in prehistoric societies. Excavations at various sites have unearthed hunting tools and weapons associated with women, such as spear points and projectile points. These discoveries challenge the notion that hunting was exclusively a male activity and suggest that women actively participated in hunting alongside men.

7.2.3 Anthropological Studies

Anthropological studies have also shed light on the role of women in hunting. Ethnographic research on contemporary hunter-gatherer societies has revealed that women often engage in hunting activities, either individually or as part of a group. These studies demonstrate that the division of labor based on gender is not a universal characteristic of human societies and that women's involvement in hunting is not a recent development.

7.2.4 Artistic Representations

Artistic representations from prehistoric times further support the idea of female hunters. Cave paintings and petroglyphs depict scenes of hunting, with both men and women shown engaging in hunting activities. These visual representations challenge the traditional narrative of gender roles and provide additional evidence of the active participation of women in hunting.

7.2.5 The Significance of Egalitarianism

The recognition of women as hunters in prehistoric societies has profound implications for our understanding of early human communities. It suggests that these societies were more egalitarian than previously believed, with both men and women contributing to the survival and success of the group. This egalitarianism extended beyond hunting and gathering activities and likely influenced other aspects of social organization, decision-making, and resource distribution.

7.2.6 Challenging Assumptions and Bias

The reevaluation of prehistoric gender roles highlights the importance of challenging assumptions and biases in archaeological research. The long-held assumption that men were the primary hunters and women were gatherers was influenced by cultural biases and modern gender norms. By recognizing and addressing these biases, researchers can gain a more accurate understanding of the past and avoid perpetuating gender stereotypes.

7.2.7 Implications for Modern Gender Equality

The recognition of women as hunters in prehistoric societies has implications for modern gender equality. It challenges the notion that certain roles and activities are inherently gendered and reinforces the idea that gender roles are socially constructed and subject to change. By understanding that women have a long history of active participation in traditionally male-dominated activities, we can challenge and dismantle gender stereotypes in contemporary society.

7.2.8 Opening New Avenues for Research

The reevaluation of prehistoric gender roles opens up new avenues for research into the lives of our ancient ancestors. It prompts us to ask new questions about the social dynamics, division of labor, and decision-making processes within early human communities. By exploring the roles and contributions of women in hunting, we can gain a more comprehensive understanding of the complexities of prehistoric societies.

7.2.9 Conclusion

The reevaluation of prehistoric gender roles challenges long-held assumptions and provides a more accurate understanding of our ancient ancestors. The evidence of female hunters highlights the egalitarian nature of early human societies and emphasizes the importance of recognizing women's contributions to the survival and success of these communities. By reevaluating prehistoric gender roles, we can foster a more inclusive and equitable understanding of our shared human history.

7.3 The Role of Bias in Research

Research in any field is susceptible to bias, and the study of prehistoric gender roles is no exception. Bias can arise from various sources, including cultural, societal, and personal beliefs, which can influence the interpretation of archaeological evidence and the conclusions drawn from it. In the context of understanding the role of women as hunters in prehistoric societies, it is crucial to acknowledge and address these biases to ensure a more accurate and inclusive understanding of our ancient ancestors.

7.3.1 Cultural and Societal Bias

Cultural and societal biases have played a significant role in shaping our understanding of prehistoric gender roles. For centuries, the prevailing belief was that men were the primary hunters, while women were confined to domestic tasks such as gathering and childcare. This bias was rooted in the patriarchal structures of many societies, where men held positions of power and authority.

These biases have influenced archaeological interpretations, leading to the marginalization and underrepresentation of women's roles as hunters. The assumption that men were the sole hunters has resulted in the overlooking of evidence that challenges this narrative. As a result, the contributions of women as hunters have been downplayed or even ignored.

7.3.2 Confirmation Bias

Confirmation bias is another factor that can influence research outcomes. Researchers may have preconceived notions about prehistoric gender roles, leading them to selectively interpret evidence that supports their beliefs while disregarding contradictory findings. This bias can hinder the objective analysis of archaeological data and limit the exploration of alternative interpretations.

To overcome confirmation bias, it is essential for researchers to approach their studies with an open mind and a willingness to challenge existing assumptions. By actively seeking out diverse perspectives and considering all available evidence, researchers can mitigate the impact of confirmation bias and arrive at more comprehensive and accurate conclusions.

7.3.3 Interpretive Bias

Interpretive bias occurs when researchers impose their own cultural or societal values onto the interpretation of archaeological evidence. This bias can lead to the misrepresentation or misinterpretation of the roles and contributions of women in prehistoric societies. For example, if a researcher holds the belief that women are inherently nurturing and passive, they may interpret evidence of female hunters as exceptions rather than the norm.

To address interpretive bias, it is crucial for researchers to adopt a culturally sensitive and contextually informed approach. This involves considering the social, economic, and environmental factors that shaped prehistoric societies and recognizing that gender roles may have varied across different cultures and time periods. By embracing a more nuanced understanding of gender dynamics, researchers can avoid imposing modern biases onto the interpretation of ancient societies.

7.3.4 Addressing Bias in Research

Recognizing and addressing bias in research is essential for developing a more accurate understanding of prehistoric gender roles. To mitigate bias, researchers can employ various strategies:

1. Diverse Research Teams: Collaborating with researchers from diverse backgrounds can help challenge biases and bring different perspectives to the research process.
2. Intersectionality: Considering the intersectionality of gender with other social categories, such as race, class, and age, can provide a more comprehensive understanding of prehistoric societies and the roles of women within them.
3. Multidisciplinary Approaches: Incorporating multiple disciplines, such as archaeology, anthropology, paleontology, and genetics, can provide a more holistic understanding of prehistoric gender roles and reduce the influence of individual biases.
4. Critical Self-Reflection: Researchers should critically reflect on their own biases and assumptions throughout the research process. This self-awareness can help identify and challenge personal biases that may impact the interpretation of evidence.
5. Open Dialogue and Peer Review: Engaging in open dialogue and subjecting research to rigorous peer review can help identify and address biases. Constructive criticism and feedback from peers can contribute to a more robust and unbiased interpretation of the evidence.

By actively addressing bias in research, we can move towards a more inclusive and accurate understanding of prehistoric gender roles, including the recognition of women as hunters in ancient societies.

7.4 Implications for Modern Gender Equality

The exploration of prehistoric gender roles and the recognition of women as hunters have significant implications for modern gender equality. The findings challenge traditional notions of gender roles and provide a historical basis for advocating for more inclusive and egalitarian societies. This section will discuss the implications of these discoveries and their relevance to contemporary gender equality movements.

7.4.1 Redefining Gender Roles

The recognition of women as hunters in prehistoric societies challenges the notion that gender roles are fixed and biologically determined. It highlights the fluidity and variability of gender roles throughout history and across cultures. By acknowledging the existence of female hunters in the past, we challenge the idea that certain activities or professions are inherently masculine or feminine. This redefinition of gender roles can contribute to breaking down gender stereotypes and promoting gender equality in modern society.

7.4.2 Empowering Women

The discovery of female hunters in prehistoric societies can serve as a source of empowerment for women today. It provides historical evidence that women have always been capable of engaging in physically demanding and traditionally male-dominated activities. By recognizing the hunting prowess of ancient women, we can inspire and empower women to pursue their passions and break through societal barriers that limit their opportunities. This newfound understanding can contribute to the dismantling of gender-based discrimination and the promotion of gender equality.

7.4.3 Challenging Gender Norms

The recognition of women as hunters challenges traditional gender norms and expectations. It highlights the diversity of human experiences and challenges the idea that there is a single "correct" way to be a man or a woman. By acknowledging the existence of female hunters in prehistoric societies, we challenge the binary understanding of gender and open up space for more fluid and inclusive gender identities. This has implications for modern discussions around gender identity, transgender rights, and the acceptance of non-binary individuals.

7.4.4 Rethinking Work and Family Dynamics

The recognition of women as hunters in prehistoric societies also has implications for rethinking work and family dynamics in modern society. It challenges the assumption that women are primarily responsible for caregiving and domestic tasks, while men are the primary breadwinners. By acknowledging the historical existence of female hunters, we can challenge the gendered division of labor and promote more equitable sharing of responsibilities within families. This can contribute to the creation of more supportive and egalitarian family structures, where both men and women have the opportunity to pursue their professional aspirations and engage in caregiving.

7.4.5 Inspiring Gender Equality Movements

The recognition of women as hunters in prehistoric societies can serve as a source of inspiration for contemporary gender equality movements. It provides historical evidence that challenges the status quo and encourages the pursuit of more inclusive and egalitarian societies. By highlighting the achievements and capabilities of women in the past, we can inspire individuals and communities to advocate for gender equality in various spheres of life, including education, employment, politics, and social interactions.

7.4.6 Promoting Diversity and Inclusion

The recognition of women as hunters in prehistoric societies promotes diversity and inclusion by expanding our understanding of human capabilities and experiences. It challenges the idea that there is a single, normative way of being a human and recognizes the richness and complexity of human diversity. By acknowledging the historical existence of female hunters, we can foster a more inclusive society that values and celebrates the contributions of individuals from all genders and backgrounds.

7.4.7 Shaping Future Research and Policy

The recognition of women as hunters in prehistoric societies has the potential to shape future research and policy agendas. It calls for a reevaluation of existing archaeological interpretations and encourages the inclusion of diverse perspectives in research. This can lead to a more comprehensive understanding of prehistoric societies and the factors that shaped human evolution. Furthermore, the recognition of women as hunters can inform policy discussions around gender equality, challenging discriminatory practices and promoting more inclusive policies in areas such as education, employment, and social welfare.

In conclusion, the recognition of women as hunters in prehistoric societies has profound implications for modern gender equality. It challenges traditional gender roles, empowers women, and promotes diversity and inclusion. By acknowledging the historical existence of female hunters, we can inspire and shape more inclusive and egalitarian societies. This newfound understanding calls for a reevaluation of existing norms, policies, and research agendas, paving the way for a more equitable future.

8

Chapter 8

The Huntress in Modern Society

8.1 Women in Contemporary Hunting Communities

In exploring the role of women in contemporary hunting communities, we can gain valuable insights into the legacy of female hunters and the impact of prehistoric gender roles on modern society. While the focus of this book has primarily been on the ancient huntresses of the past, it is essential to acknowledge the presence and contributions of women in hunting communities today.

8.1.1 The Changing Landscape of Hunting

Over the years, the perception of hunting as a predominantly male activity has been challenged. In many parts of the world, women are actively participating in hunting activities, both as individuals and as members of hunting groups. This shift in gender dynamics within hunting communities reflects the changing societal norms and the empowerment of women in various domains.

8.1.2 Women as Skilled Hunters

Contrary to traditional gender stereotypes, women have proven themselves to be skilled hunters in contemporary hunting communities. They have demonstrated proficiency in using various hunting techniques and tools, adapting to different environments, and contributing to the success of group hunts. The inclusion of women in hunting activities has not only diversified the skill set within these communities but has also challenged the notion that hunting is exclusively a male domain.

8.1.3 The Benefits of Female Hunters

The presence of women in contemporary hunting communities has brought about numerous benefits. Firstly, it has fostered a sense of equality and inclusivity within these communities, promoting a more balanced and harmonious environment. Secondly, the involvement of women has expanded the knowledge base and skill repertoire of hunting groups, leading to increased efficiency and success in hunts. Lastly, the participation of women in hunting has provided them with a platform to challenge societal norms and break free from traditional gender roles.

8.1.4 Challenges and Opportunities

While the inclusion of women in hunting communities has been a positive development, it has not been without its challenges. Deep-rooted gender stereotypes and societal expectations can still hinder the full participation of women in hunting activities. Additionally, the historical underrepresentation of women in hunting has resulted in a lack of role models and mentors for aspiring female hunters. However, these challenges also present opportunities for further research and advocacy to promote gender equality in hunting communities.

8.1.5 The Impact on Modern Gender Norms

The recognition of women as hunters in contemporary society has significant implications for modern gender norms. It challenges the traditional division of labor based on gender and highlights the importance of recognizing and valuing the diverse contributions of individuals, regardless of their gender. By acknowledging the historical presence of female hunters, we can reshape societal perceptions and promote a more inclusive understanding of gender roles.

8.1.6 Empowering Recognizing Female Hunting Legacies

The acknowledgment and celebration of female hunting legacies empower women in contemporary society. By recognizing the historical agency and capabilities of women as hunters, we provide a platform for women to reclaim their place in hunting communities and challenge the limitations imposed by gender stereotypes. This empowerment extends beyond the realm of hunting and contributes to the broader movement for gender equality and women's empowerment.

8.1.7 Inspiring Future Generations

The visibility of women in contemporary hunting communities serves as an inspiration for future generations. By showcasing the achievements and capabilities of female hunters, we challenge the notion that certain activities are inherently gendered. This can encourage young girls and women to pursue their passions, break free from societal expectations, and explore traditionally male-dominated fields.

8.1.8 The Future of Gender Studies in Archaeology

The recognition of women as hunters in contemporary hunting communities also has implications for the future of gender studies in archaeology. It highlights the importance of revisiting and reevaluating existing archaeological evidence and interpretations to ensure a more accurate understanding of prehistoric gender roles. It also emphasizes the need for interdisciplinary approaches and collaborative research to uncover the untold stories of women in ancient societies.

In conclusion, the presence and contributions of women in contemporary hunting communities challenge traditional gender roles and provide valuable insights into the legacy of female hunters. By recognizing and celebrating the agency and capabilities of women as hunters, we empower women in modern society and pave the way for a more inclusive understanding of prehistoric gender roles. The journey towards gender equality continues, and the recognition of female hunting legacies is a significant step forward in this ongoing endeavor.

8.2 The Influence of Prehistoric Gender Roles on Modern Gender Norms

Throughout history, gender roles have played a significant role in shaping societal norms and expectations. The conventional understanding of prehistoric gender roles has often depicted men as hunters and women as gatherers, reinforcing the notion that women were confined to domestic tasks while men engaged in more physically demanding activities. However, recent research and archaeological findings have challenged this long-held assumption, revealing a more complex and egalitarian picture of our ancient ancestors.

8.2.1 Rethinking Prehistoric Gender Roles

The discovery of archaeological evidence and the reevaluation of existing data have shed light on the active role that women played as hunters in prehistoric societies. This new understanding challenges the traditional narrative that women were solely gatherers and highlights the importance of recognizing the diverse roles that both men and women played in early human communities.

8.2.2 The Impact of Prehistoric Gender Roles on Modern Norms

The influence of prehistoric gender roles on modern gender norms cannot be understated. For centuries, the belief in inherent gender differences and the division of labor based on these assumptions have shaped societal expectations and limited opportunities for women. The recognition of women as hunters in prehistoric times challenges these deeply ingrained beliefs and provides a historical precedent for gender equality.

8.2.3 Breaking Down Stereotypes

The revelation that women were active hunters challenges the stereotype that hunting was exclusively a male domain. It demonstrates that gender roles were not fixed or universal throughout history but varied across different cultures and time periods. This understanding encourages us to question and challenge the gender stereotypes that persist in modern society, promoting a more inclusive and egalitarian view of gender roles.

8.2.4 Redefining Masculinity and Femininity

The recognition of women as hunters in prehistoric societies also prompts a reevaluation of traditional notions of masculinity and femininity. The idea that physical strength and aggression are exclusively masculine traits is undermined by the evidence of women engaging in hunting activities. This challenges the binary understanding of gender and encourages a more fluid and nuanced understanding of what it means to be masculine or feminine.

8.2.5 Empowering Women

The discovery of female hunters in prehistoric societies has the potential to empower women in modern society. By highlighting the historical precedent of women engaging in physically demanding tasks, it challenges the notion that certain activities are inherently gendered. This recognition can inspire women to pursue their passions and interests, regardless of societal expectations or gender norms.

8.2.6 Shaping Gender Equality Movements

The recognition of women as hunters in prehistoric times has significant implications for the gender equality movement. It provides historical evidence that challenges the notion of male superiority and reinforces the idea that gender roles are socially constructed rather than biologically determined. This understanding can fuel the ongoing fight for gender equality and serve as a powerful tool in dismantling gender-based discrimination and stereotypes.

8.2.7 Inspiring Future Research

The revelation of women as hunters in prehistoric societies opens up new avenues for research and exploration. It encourages scholars to delve deeper into the lives of our ancient ancestors, seeking to understand the complexities of their social structures, the division of labor, and the dynamics of gender roles. This research can provide valuable insights into the evolution of human societies and contribute to a more comprehensive understanding of our shared history.

8.2.8 Challenging Assumptions and Moving Forward

The recognition of women as hunters in prehistoric societies challenges long-held assumptions about gender roles and provides a more inclusive understanding of our ancient ancestors. It encourages us to question the limitations imposed by societal norms and expectations, promoting a more equitable and diverse society. By embracing the influence of prehistoric gender roles on modern gender norms, we can move towards a future that celebrates the contributions and capabilities of all individuals, regardless of their gender.

8.3 The Empowerment of Recognizing Female Hunting Legacies

Throughout history, women have often been portrayed as passive participants in prehistoric societies, confined to domestic roles and excluded from activities such as hunting. However, recent research and archaeological discoveries have shed light on the significant role that women played as hunters in ancient societies. Recognizing and acknowledging the legacy of female hunters is not only empowering for women today but also challenges traditional gender norms and provides a more inclusive understanding of prehistoric gender roles.

8.3.1 Breaking Stereotypes and Empowering Women

The recognition of female hunting legacies has the power to break down long-standing stereotypes and empower women in modern society. By highlighting the historical evidence of women as skilled hunters, we challenge the notion that hunting was exclusively a male domain. This recognition allows women to reclaim their place in history and assert their capabilities in traditionally male-dominated activities.

Understanding the historical role of female hunters also provides a sense of empowerment for women today. It demonstrates that women have always possessed the skills, strength, and courage necessary for hunting, debunking the notion that these qualities are inherently male. By recognizing and celebrating the hunting legacies of women, we inspire women to pursue their passions and break free from societal expectations.

8.3.2 Redefining Gender Norms and Roles

The recognition of female hunting legacies forces us to reconsider traditional gender norms and roles. It challenges the notion that gender roles have always been fixed and immutable throughout history. Instead, it reveals that prehistoric societies were more egalitarian than previously believed, with men and women sharing responsibilities and contributing equally to their communities' survival.

By acknowledging the historical presence of female hunters, we redefine what it means to be a woman in society. We move away from the restrictive and limiting stereotypes that have confined women to domestic roles and recognize their capacity for strength, resilience, and leadership. This redefinition of gender norms allows for greater gender equality and inclusivity in contemporary society.

8.3.3 Inspiring Future Generations

Recognizing the legacy of female hunters not only empowers women today but also inspires future generations. By showcasing the historical achievements of women in hunting, we provide young girls with role models who defy societal expectations and demonstrate that they can excel in any field they choose.

The recognition of female hunting legacies also encourages young boys to challenge traditional gender norms and embrace a more inclusive understanding of masculinity. It teaches them that strength and courage are not exclusive to men and that women have always been capable of extraordinary feats.

8.3.4 Preserving Cultural Heritage

Acknowledging the historical contributions of female hunters is crucial for preserving our cultural heritage. By recognizing the role of women in hunting, we ensure that their stories are not lost or forgotten. This recognition allows us to appreciate the diversity and complexity of prehistoric societies and fosters a deeper understanding of our shared human history.

Preserving the cultural heritage of female hunters also helps us challenge biased interpretations of archaeological evidence. By acknowledging the presence of women in hunting activities, we avoid perpetuating gender biases that have influenced previous research and interpretations. This leads to a more accurate and comprehensive understanding of prehistoric societies.

8.3.5 Promoting Gender Equality

The recognition of female hunting legacies has broader implications for promoting gender equality in modern society. By challenging traditional gender roles and highlighting the historical contributions of women, we advocate for equal opportunities and rights for all genders.

This recognition encourages us to question and dismantle the gender biases that persist in various aspects of society, including education, employment, and leadership. It promotes a more inclusive and equitable society where individuals are not limited by their gender but are valued for their skills, abilities, and contributions.

8.3.6 Conclusion

The empowerment that comes from recognizing the legacies of female hunters is transformative. It challenges long-held assumptions, redefines gender norms, and inspires future generations. By acknowledging the historical role of women in hunting, we not only empower women today but also promote a more inclusive and equal society. The recognition of female hunting legacies is a crucial step towards a more comprehensive understanding of prehistoric gender roles and a more equitable future for all.

8.4 The Future of Gender Studies in Archaeology

As our understanding of prehistoric gender roles continues to evolve, the future of gender studies in archaeology holds great promise. The recent discoveries challenging traditional assumptions about the roles of men and women in ancient societies have opened up new avenues for research and exploration. This section will discuss the potential directions that gender studies in archaeology may take in the coming years, as well as the implications for our understanding of human history and modern gender equality.

8.4.1 Interdisciplinary Approaches

One of the key aspects of the future of gender studies in archaeology lies in the adoption of interdisciplinary approaches. By combining the expertise of archaeologists, anthropologists, historians, geneticists, and other related fields, we can gain a more comprehensive understanding of prehistoric gender roles. Collaborative research projects that bring together scholars from various disciplines can shed light on different aspects of ancient societies, including the roles and contributions of women as hunters.

8.4.2 Technological Advancements

Advancements in archaeological techniques and technologies also hold great potential for future gender studies. As new methods of analysis emerge, such as DNA analysis and isotopic studies, we can gain insights into the biological sex of ancient individuals and their dietary patterns. These advancements can help us identify female hunters and further support the growing body of evidence challenging traditional gender roles.

Additionally, the use of remote sensing technologies, such as LiDAR (Light Detection and Ranging), can aid in the discovery of previously unknown archaeological sites. This can provide us with a broader dataset to examine and analyze the presence and activities of female hunters in different regions and time periods.

8.4.3 Exploring Other Aspects of Prehistoric Gender Roles

While the focus of this book has been on the role of women as hunters, there are still many other aspects of prehistoric gender roles that warrant further exploration. Future research could delve into the division of labor within ancient societies, the social and economic implications of gender roles, and the impact of gender on the development of cultural practices and traditions.

By examining these various aspects, we can gain a more nuanced understanding of the complexities of prehistoric gender roles and challenge any lingering biases or assumptions that may persist.

8.4.4 Addressing Bias and Assumptions

As we move forward in our understanding of prehistoric gender roles, it is crucial to address any biases and assumptions that may influence our interpretations. Recognizing and challenging these biases can help us develop a more accurate and inclusive understanding of ancient societies.

Archaeologists and researchers must remain vigilant in their efforts to avoid projecting modern gender norms onto the past. By critically examining the evidence and considering alternative interpretations, we can ensure that our conclusions are based on sound research and not influenced by preconceived notions.

8.4.5 The Importance of Education and Outreach

The future of gender studies in archaeology also relies on education and outreach. It is essential to disseminate the findings and insights gained from this research to a wider audience, including the general public, students, and policymakers. By raising awareness about the diverse roles and contributions of women in ancient societies, we can challenge gender stereotypes and promote a more inclusive understanding of human history.

Educational initiatives, museum exhibits, and public lectures can play a crucial role in sharing this knowledge and fostering a greater appreciation for the complexity of prehistoric gender roles. By engaging with the public, we can inspire future generations of archaeologists and researchers to continue exploring and challenging our understanding of the past.

8.4.6 Implications for Modern Gender Equality

The future of gender studies in archaeology has significant implications for modern gender equality. By recognizing the historical presence of female hunters and challenging traditional gender roles, we can contribute to the ongoing fight for gender equality in contemporary society.

Understanding that women played active roles in hunting and other traditionally male-dominated activities can help dismantle harmful stereotypes and promote a more inclusive society. By acknowledging the egalitarian nature of our ancient ancestors, we can challenge the notion that gender inequality is inherent or natural.

In conclusion, the future of gender studies in archaeology holds great potential for further unraveling the complexities of prehistoric gender roles. Through interdisciplinary approaches, technological advancements, and a commitment to addressing bias and assumptions, we can continue to challenge and transform our understanding of ancient societies. By sharing this knowledge and promoting a more inclusive understanding of prehistoric gender roles, we can contribute to the ongoing pursuit of gender equality in modern society.

9

Chapter 9

Unanswered Questions and Future Research

9.1 Remaining Gaps in the Evidence

As we delve deeper into the research and evidence surrounding the role of women as hunters in prehistoric societies, it becomes evident that there are still some gaps in our understanding. While significant progress has been made in challenging traditional gender roles and shedding light on the hunting prowess of ancient women, there are still unanswered questions that require further investigation. In this section, we will explore some of these remaining gaps in the evidence and discuss the potential avenues for future research.

9.1.1 The Elusiveness of Direct Evidence

One of the primary challenges in studying prehistoric gender roles is the scarcity of direct evidence. The archaeological record often lacks clear and unambiguous indicators of female hunting activities. This absence of direct evidence makes it difficult to ascertain the extent of women's involvement in hunting and the specific roles they played. While some archaeological sites have provided tantalizing hints, such as the presence of female-specific hunting tools or the remains of female individuals with hunting-related injuries, these findings are relatively rare and localized.

To bridge this gap, future research could focus on developing new methodologies and techniques that can identify subtle traces of female hunting activities. This may involve analyzing microscopic wear patterns on tools, studying the chemical composition of residues on hunting implements, or exploring the potential use of biomolecular analysis to identify gender-specific markers in ancient skeletal remains. By employing innovative approaches, we can hope to uncover more direct evidence of women's participation in hunting.

9.1.2 Regional and Temporal Variations

Another area that requires further exploration is the regional and temporal variations in prehistoric gender roles. The existing research has primarily focused on specific regions and time periods, such as the Upper Paleolithic in Europe or the Americas. While these studies have provided valuable insights, they may not represent a comprehensive picture of prehistoric gender dynamics across different geographical areas and timeframes.

Future research should aim to expand the scope of investigation to include a wider range of regions and time periods. By examining diverse archaeological contexts, we can gain a more nuanced understanding of how gender roles may have varied across different societies and environments. This comparative approach will help us identify common patterns and unique cultural practices related to female hunting.

9.1.3 The Influence of Social and Environmental Factors

Understanding the factors that influenced the participation of women in hunting is another crucial aspect that requires further exploration. While it is clear that women were involved in hunting to varying degrees, the specific social and environmental factors that shaped their roles remain less understood. Factors such as resource availability, social organization, technological advancements, and cultural beliefs likely played a significant role in determining the extent of female hunting participation.

Future research should aim to unravel the complex interplay between these factors and the involvement of women in hunting. Comparative studies across different societies and time periods can help identify commonalities and differences in the social and environmental contexts that influenced female hunting. Additionally, interdisciplinary approaches that integrate archaeological, anthropological, and ecological perspectives can provide a more comprehensive understanding of the multifaceted factors at play.

9.1.4 Exploring Non-Hunting Aspects of Gender Roles

While the focus of this book has primarily been on the hunting activities of women, it is essential to acknowledge that gender roles in prehistoric societies encompassed a wide range of activities beyond hunting and gathering. Future research should aim to explore other aspects of gender roles, such as the division of labor in domestic tasks, childcare, and ritual practices. By examining the broader spectrum of gendered activities, we can gain a more holistic understanding of prehistoric gender dynamics.

This exploration should also consider the potential intersections between different gendered activities. For example, how did women's involvement in hunting intersect with their roles as gatherers or caregivers? Did these roles overlap or complement each other? By investigating these questions, we can develop a more nuanced understanding of the complex web of gender roles in prehistoric societies.

In conclusion, while significant progress has been made in challenging traditional gender roles and highlighting the hunting contributions of women in prehistoric societies, there are still gaps in our understanding. The scarcity of direct evidence, regional and temporal variations, the influence of social and environmental factors, and the exploration of non-hunting aspects of gender roles all present avenues for future research. By addressing these gaps, we can continue to refine our understanding of prehistoric gender dynamics and gain a more comprehensive view of our ancient ancestors' lives.

9.2 Exploring Other Aspects of Prehistoric Gender Roles

As our understanding of prehistoric gender roles continues to evolve, it is crucial to explore other aspects beyond the traditional dichotomy of men as hunters and women as gatherers. The recent findings challenging these assumptions have shed light on the complexity and diversity of gender roles in ancient societies. This chapter delves into various aspects of prehistoric gender roles, examining the multifaceted nature of human societies and the roles women played in them.

9.2.1 Economic Contributions

While hunting has received significant attention in the discussion of prehistoric gender roles, it is essential to recognize that economic contributions extended beyond hunting and gathering. Recent research has revealed evidence of women engaging in various economic activities, such as tool production, craft specialization, and resource management. These findings suggest that women played a more active role in shaping their communities' economic systems than previously assumed.

9.2.2 Ritual and Spiritual Practices

Exploring prehistoric gender roles also involves investigating the role of women in ritual and spiritual practices. Archaeological evidence has uncovered artifacts and burial sites that indicate women's involvement in religious ceremonies and rituals. These findings challenge the notion that religious and spiritual domains were exclusively male-dominated, highlighting the importance of women in shaping the spiritual beliefs and practices of ancient societies.

9.2.3 Social Organization and Power Structures

Understanding prehistoric gender roles requires an examination of social organization and power structures within ancient communities. Recent research has revealed that women held positions of authority and played significant roles in decision-making processes. This challenges the traditional assumption that power was solely concentrated in the hands of men. By exploring the social dynamics of ancient societies, we gain a more nuanced understanding of the complex power structures that existed and the contributions women made to shaping their communities.

9.2.4 Parenting and Childcare

Another aspect of prehistoric gender roles that warrants exploration is parenting and childcare. Recent studies have suggested that women played a crucial role in child-rearing and nurturing within ancient societies. The division of labor in childcare might have been more equitable than previously assumed, with both men and women actively involved in raising and caring for children. By examining the archaeological record and anthropological studies, we can gain insights into the diverse ways in which ancient societies approached parenting and childcare.

9.2.5 Artistic and Creative Expressions

Artistic and creative expressions provide another avenue for exploring prehistoric gender roles. By analyzing cave paintings, sculptures, and other forms of ancient art, we can uncover representations of women and their roles in society. Recent research has revealed depictions of women engaged in hunting, suggesting that artistic expressions served as a means to celebrate and honor the contributions of female hunters. By examining these artistic representations, we gain a deeper understanding of the cultural significance and recognition of women's roles in prehistoric societies.

9.2.6 Trade and Exchange Networks

Investigating prehistoric gender roles also involves exploring trade and exchange networks. Recent archaeological discoveries have highlighted the active participation of women in long-distance trade and exchange. Women played a crucial role in facilitating the movement of goods, ideas, and cultural practices across different regions. By examining the archaeological evidence of trade networks, we can gain insights into the economic and social roles women played in ancient societies.

9.2.7 Technological Innovations and Inventions

Exploring prehistoric gender roles also requires an examination of technological innovations and inventions. Recent research has revealed that women were not passive recipients of technological advancements but actively contributed to the development and refinement of tools and technologies. By studying the archaeological record, we can uncover the contributions of women to technological innovations, challenging the notion that technological advancements were solely driven by men.

9.2.8 Environmental Adaptation and Resource Management

Understanding prehistoric gender roles also involves exploring how ancient societies adapted to their environments and managed resources. Recent research has highlighted the active role women played in environmental adaptation and resource management. Women's knowledge of local ecosystems and their expertise in gathering and utilizing resources were crucial for the survival and well-being of their communities. By examining the archaeological and anthropological evidence, we can gain insights into the ways in which women contributed to environmental sustainability and resource management.

In conclusion, exploring other aspects of prehistoric gender roles beyond hunting and gathering provides a more comprehensive understanding of the complexity and diversity of ancient societies. By examining economic contributions, ritual practices, social organization, parenting, artistic expressions, trade networks, technological innovations, and environmental adaptation, we gain insights into the multifaceted roles women played in shaping their communities. This expanded perspective challenges long-held assumptions and opens new avenues for research, ultimately contributing to a more inclusive understanding of prehistoric gender roles.

9.3 Advancements in Archaeological Techniques and Technologies

As the study of prehistoric gender roles continues to evolve, advancements in archaeological techniques and technologies have played a crucial role in uncovering new evidence and challenging long-held assumptions. These advancements have allowed researchers to delve deeper into the lives of our ancient ancestors and shed light on the true nature of prehistoric societies. In this section, we will explore some of the key advancements that have revolutionized our understanding of prehistoric gender roles.

9.3.1 Radiocarbon Dating and Chronology

One of the most significant advancements in archaeological techniques is the development of radiocarbon dating. This method allows researchers to determine the age of organic materials, such as bones and charcoal, with remarkable accuracy. By analyzing the decay of radioactive carbon isotopes, archaeologists can establish the chronology of ancient sites and artifacts.

Radiocarbon dating has been instrumental in providing precise dates for archaeological finds related to hunting activities. By dating hunting tools, animal remains, and hunting-related artifacts, researchers have been able to establish a timeline of female hunting practices throughout history. This has allowed for a more nuanced understanding of the role of women in hunting and has challenged the notion that hunting was exclusively a male activity.

9.3.2 Zooarchaeology and Faunal Analysis

Zooarchaeology, the study of animal remains found at archaeological sites, has also contributed significantly to our understanding of prehistoric gender roles. By analyzing the bones and teeth of animals, researchers can determine the species, age, and sex of the animals hunted by ancient humans.

Faunal analysis has revealed that women were actively involved in hunting, as evidenced by the presence of female-specific hunting tools and the hunting of female animals. This challenges the traditional assumption that hunting was solely a male domain. By examining the distribution of hunting tools and the types of animals hunted, researchers have been able to reconstruct the hunting strategies employed by ancient women.

9.3.3 Microscopic Analysis and Residue Analysis

Microscopic analysis and residue analysis have provided valuable insights into the use of hunting tools and the activities performed by ancient individuals. Microscopic analysis involves the examination of tool surfaces under high magnification to identify traces of use-wear, such as cut marks and polish. Residue analysis, on the other hand, involves the identification of organic residues, such as blood, fat, and plant materials, on the surfaces of tools.

These techniques have revealed that hunting tools attributed to women show similar use-wear patterns and residue traces as those attributed to men. This suggests that women were actively engaged in hunting activities and were not limited to gathering or domestic tasks. The use of hunting tools by women challenges the traditional gender roles assigned to prehistoric societies and highlights the egalitarian nature of early human communities.

9.3.4 DNA Analysis and Isotopic Studies

Advancements in DNA analysis and isotopic studies have provided further evidence of the involvement of women in hunting activities. By analyzing ancient DNA extracted from skeletal remains, researchers can determine the sex of individuals and identify genetic markers associated with hunting-related traits.

Isotopic studies, which analyze the chemical composition of bones and teeth, can provide insights into an individual's diet and mobility patterns. By comparing the isotopic signatures of male and female individuals, researchers have found that women exhibited similar isotopic profiles to men, indicating a shared diet that included animal protein obtained through hunting.

These studies challenge the notion that women were solely responsible for gathering plant-based foods and highlight their active participation in hunting and the acquisition of animal resources.

9.3.5 Geographic Information Systems (GIS) and Spatial Analysis

Geographic Information Systems (GIS) and spatial analysis have revolutionized the way researchers study ancient landscapes and human behavior. By integrating archaeological data with geographic data, researchers can analyze patterns of site distribution, resource availability, and mobility patterns.

GIS has allowed researchers to identify hunting territories and track the movements of ancient hunting groups. By mapping the distribution of hunting tools and animal remains, researchers have been able to reconstruct the spatial organization of hunting activities and identify areas where women played a significant role in hunting.

These advancements in archaeological techniques and technologies have provided a more comprehensive understanding of prehistoric gender roles. By challenging long-held assumptions and uncovering new evidence, researchers have revealed the active participation of women in hunting activities. These advancements have not only transformed our understanding of prehistoric societies but also have broader implications for our understanding of gender equality and the evolution of human societies.

9.4 Collaborative Research and Interdisciplinary Approaches

In order to fully understand and explore the lives of our ancient ancestors, it is crucial to adopt collaborative research and interdisciplinary approaches. The study of prehistoric gender roles requires the expertise and insights of various disciplines, including archaeology, anthropology, paleontology, and sociology. By combining these different fields of study, researchers can gain a more comprehensive understanding of the complex dynamics of prehistoric societies and the roles of women as hunters.

9.4.1 Interdisciplinary Collaboration

Interdisciplinary collaboration allows researchers to approach the study of prehistoric gender roles from multiple perspectives. By bringing together experts from different fields, such as archaeologists, anthropologists, and paleontologists, a more holistic understanding of the past can be achieved. For example, archaeologists can provide insights into the material culture and artifacts associated with hunting, while anthropologists can analyze the social and cultural aspects of hunting practices. Paleontologists can contribute by studying fossil evidence and providing insights into the physical capabilities of ancient humans.

Collaboration between these disciplines can help bridge gaps in knowledge and provide a more nuanced understanding of prehistoric gender roles. By pooling their expertise and resources, researchers can uncover new evidence and challenge existing assumptions about the roles of women in ancient societies.

9.4.2 Technological Advancements

Advancements in archaeological techniques and technologies have greatly enhanced our ability to study prehistoric gender roles. The use of advanced imaging techniques, such as ground-penetrating radar and LiDAR (Light Detection and Ranging), allows researchers to uncover hidden archaeological features and gain a better understanding of ancient landscapes. These technologies can help identify hunting sites, track migration patterns, and reveal the presence of female hunters.

Additionally, the analysis of ancient DNA has provided valuable insights into the genetic makeup of ancient populations. By studying the genetic material preserved in ancient remains, researchers can determine the sex of individuals and explore the genetic diversity within prehistoric communities. This information can help shed light on the roles and contributions of women in hunting activities.

9.4.3 Ethnographic Studies

Ethnographic studies of modern hunter-gatherer societies can also provide valuable insights into prehistoric gender roles. By observing and interacting with contemporary hunter-gatherer communities, researchers can gain a better understanding of the social dynamics and division of labor within these societies. Ethnographic studies have shown that in many modern hunter-gatherer societies, women actively participate in hunting activities alongside men, challenging the notion that hunting was exclusively a male domain in prehistoric times.

By comparing the behaviors and roles of modern hunter-gatherer societies with archaeological evidence, researchers can make informed interpretations about the roles of women in prehistoric hunting. This interdisciplinary approach allows for a more nuanced understanding of prehistoric gender roles and challenges the traditional assumptions that have long portrayed women as passive gatherers.

9.4.4 Collaborative Fieldwork

Collaborative fieldwork is another important aspect of researching pre-historic gender roles. By working together in the field, researchers from different disciplines can combine their expertise and perspectives to gather and interpret data. This collaborative approach ensures that multiple viewpoints are considered and that a more comprehensive understanding of prehistoric societies is achieved.

Fieldwork can involve excavations, surveys, and the collection of artifacts and samples for analysis. By working together, researchers can identify potential hunting sites, analyze the distribution of artifacts, and reconstruct the activities and behaviors of ancient hunters. This collaborative fieldwork not only enhances the quality of research but also fosters a greater sense of teamwork and shared knowledge among researchers.

9.4.5 Community Engagement

Engaging with local communities and indigenous peoples is crucial for conducting ethical and inclusive research on prehistoric gender roles. By involving community members in the research process, researchers can gain valuable insights and perspectives that may have been overlooked. This collaborative approach ensures that the voices and knowledge of local communities are respected and incorporated into the research.

Community engagement also allows researchers to share their findings with the public and raise awareness about the importance of understanding prehistoric gender roles. By disseminating research findings through public lectures, exhibitions, and educational programs, researchers can promote a more inclusive understanding of the past and challenge existing stereotypes and biases.

In conclusion, collaborative research and interdisciplinary approaches are essential for unraveling the complexities of prehistoric gender roles. By combining the expertise of different disciplines, utilizing technological advancements, conducting ethnographic studies, engaging with local communities, and collaborating in fieldwork, researchers can gain a more comprehensive understanding of the lives of our ancient ancestors. This inclusive and multidisciplinary approach not only challenges long-held assumptions but also paves the way for a more accurate and inclusive understanding of prehistoric gender roles.

10

Chapter 10

Conclusion

10.1 Summary of Findings

Throughout this book, we have explored the extensive research and evidence that challenges the conventional portrayal of prehistoric gender roles. The notion that men were solely hunters and women were gatherers is being dismantled, revealing a more complex and egalitarian picture of our ancient ancestors. The findings presented in this book shed light on the significant role of women as hunters and the implications of recognizing their contributions to our understanding of prehistoric societies.

The research presented in Chapter 2, "The Huntress Unveiled," provides compelling archaeological, paleontological, and anthropological evidence of female hunters. Archaeological excavations have unearthed tools and weapons associated with hunting activities, often found in close proximity to female remains. These discoveries challenge the assumption that hunting was exclusively a male domain. Paleontological studies have revealed the physical capabilities of women, such as their strength and endurance, which would have been advantageous for hunting. Anthropological studies have documented the presence of female hunters in various indigenous societies, further supporting the idea that women played an active role in hunting.

Chapter 3, "Hunting Techniques and Tools," delves into the specific techniques and tools utilized by ancient huntresses. The evidence suggests that women developed their own hunting implements, such as spears, bows, and traps, tailored to their physical abilities. They employed various hunting strategies and tactics, adapting to different environments and prey. The role of women in group hunts was not limited to gathering or supporting roles but extended to active participation in the hunt itself. This challenges the traditional notion of gender roles within hunting groups.

In Chapter 4, "The Social Dynamics of Hunting," we explore the cooperative nature of hunting and the impact of female hunters on group dynamics. Hunting was a collective endeavor, requiring coordination, communication, and decision-making. The presence of female hunters would have influenced the dynamics of these groups, challenging traditional gender roles and potentially contributing to a more egalitarian society. Leadership and decision-making within hunting groups were not solely the domain of men, as women would have played crucial roles in guiding and organizing hunts.

Chapter 5, "Hunting and Survival," examines the importance of hunting for early humans and the role of female hunters in ensuring group survival. Hunting provided essential resources, such as meat and animal byproducts, which contributed to the nutritional needs of the group. The ability of women to contribute to hunting would have increased the overall success rate of hunts, ensuring the survival and well-being of the community. Furthermore, the challenges posed by hunting would have stimulated the development of cognitive abilities, potentially contributing to the evolution of human intelligence.

In Chapter 6, "Artistic Representations of Female Hunters," we explore the depictions of female hunters in ancient art. Cave paintings and petroglyphs provide visual evidence of women engaged in hunting activities, challenging the assumption that hunting was exclusively a male domain. These artistic representations carry symbolic and cultural significance, reflecting the recognition and celebration of female hunters within their respective societies. The legacy of female hunters in artistic traditions highlights their importance and influence in prehistoric societies.

Chapter 7, "Challenging Gender Stereotypes," delves into the impact of gender stereotypes on archaeological interpretations and the reevaluation of prehistoric gender roles. The biases and assumptions of past researchers have influenced the understanding of gender roles in prehistory. By challenging these biases and reevaluating the evidence, we can gain a more accurate understanding of the diverse roles played by women in ancient societies. Recognizing the contributions of female hunters has broader implications for modern gender equality, challenging societal norms and promoting a more inclusive understanding of gender roles.

In Chapter 8, "The Huntress in Modern Society," we explore the influence of prehistoric gender roles on contemporary hunting communities and the empowerment that comes from recognizing female hunting legacies. Women continue to participate in hunting activities today, and their contributions are increasingly acknowledged and valued. Understanding the historical context of female hunters provides a foundation for challenging modern gender norms and promoting equality within hunting communities and society at large.

Chapter 9, "Unanswered Questions and Future Research," acknowledges the remaining gaps in the evidence and the need for further exploration of prehistoric gender roles. Advancements in archaeological techniques and technologies offer exciting possibilities for uncovering new insights into the lives of ancient huntresses. Collaborative research and interdisciplinary approaches will be crucial in expanding our understanding of prehistoric societies and the roles of women within them.

In conclusion, the findings presented in this book challenge long-held assumptions about prehistoric gender roles and reveal the significant contributions of female hunters. Our ancient ancestors lived in egalitarian societies, where women played active roles in hunting and shaping their communities. Recognizing the importance of female hunters has implications for our understanding of prehistory, gender equality, and the broader narrative of human history. By embracing a more inclusive understanding of prehistoric gender roles, we can gain valuable insights into our shared past and pave the way for a more equitable future.

Female Hunters

The recognition of female hunters in prehistoric societies has profound implications for our understanding of ancient human cultures and the evolution of gender roles. This groundbreaking research challenges long-held assumptions about the division of labor and the roles of men and women in early human societies. By acknowledging the existence of female hunters, we gain a more comprehensive and accurate understanding of our ancient ancestors and their social dynamics. In this section, we will explore the implications of recognizing female hunters and the significance of this discovery.

10.2.1 Redefining Gender Roles

The discovery of female hunters redefines traditional gender roles in prehistoric societies. It challenges the notion that men were solely responsible for hunting while women were confined to gathering activities. This new understanding highlights the complexity and diversity of ancient human cultures, where gender roles were not fixed but varied across different societies and time periods. By recognizing the active participation of women in hunting, we challenge the binary view of gender roles and promote a more inclusive understanding of human societies.

10.2.2 Egalitarianism in Prehistoric Societies

The recognition of female hunters provides evidence for the existence of egalitarianism in prehistoric societies. It suggests that early humans lived in more egalitarian social structures, where both men and women played vital roles in securing food resources for their communities. This challenges the prevailing assumption that gender inequality and male dominance were inherent features of early human societies. The existence of female hunters indicates a more balanced distribution of labor and decision-making power, emphasizing the importance of cooperation and collaboration for survival.

10.2.3 Women's Contributions to Group Survival

The acknowledgment of female hunters sheds light on the significant contributions women made to the survival and well-being of their communities. Hunting was a crucial activity for early humans, providing them with essential protein-rich food sources. By actively participating in hunting, women played a vital role in ensuring the sustenance and survival of their groups. This recognition challenges the notion that women were solely responsible for gathering plant-based resources and highlights their agency and skill in securing animal resources.

10.2.4 Challenging Gender Stereotypes

The recognition of female hunters challenges deeply ingrained gender stereotypes that have shaped our understanding of prehistoric societies. It forces us to question the biases and assumptions that have influenced archaeological interpretations and perpetuated the notion of male dominance. By challenging these stereotypes, we create space for a more nuanced and accurate understanding of the past, free from gender biases. This has broader implications for modern gender equality, as it challenges the notion that gender roles are fixed and immutable.

10.2.5 Empowering Women's History

Recognizing female hunters empowers women's history by highlighting their agency, skills, and contributions in ancient societies. It provides a historical precedent for women's involvement in traditionally male-dominated activities and challenges the notion that women's roles have always been confined to domestic and nurturing spheres. By acknowledging the existence of female hunters, we celebrate the resilience and capabilities of women throughout history and inspire future generations to challenge gender norms and pursue their passions.

10.2.6 Reevaluating Human Evolution

The recognition of female hunters also has implications for our understanding of human evolution. It challenges the narrative that the development of hunting skills and the associated cognitive abilities were exclusively male traits. The active participation of women in hunting suggests that the evolution of intelligence and complex social behaviors was a collective endeavor, shaped by both men and women. This challenges the traditional view that male hunting prowess was the driving force behind human cognitive development.

10.2.7 Inspiring Future Research

The recognition of female hunters opens up new avenues for research into prehistoric gender roles and ancient human societies. It encourages scholars to reevaluate existing archaeological evidence and explore new sources of information that may have been overlooked or misinterpreted. This includes revisiting archaeological sites, reanalyzing artifacts, and incorporating interdisciplinary approaches to gain a more comprehensive understanding of the lives of our ancient ancestors. The recognition of female hunters also highlights the importance of collaborative research, where diverse perspectives and expertise contribute to a more holistic understanding of the past.

In conclusion, the recognition of female hunters in prehistoric societies has far-reaching implications for our understanding of ancient human cultures, gender roles, and human evolution. It challenges traditional assumptions, promotes a more inclusive understanding of the past, and empowers women's history. By recognizing the active participation of women in hunting, we gain a more comprehensive and accurate understanding of our ancient ancestors and their social dynamics. This discovery inspires future research and encourages us to question long-held assumptions, fostering a more inclusive and egalitarian understanding of prehistoric gender roles.

10.3 Lessons from Our Ancient Huntresses

Throughout this book, we have explored the evidence and research that challenges traditional assumptions about prehistoric gender roles. The discovery that women were not just gatherers but also skilled hunters has profound implications for our understanding of our ancient ancestors and the evolution of our species. In this final section, we will reflect on the lessons we can learn from our ancient huntresses and the importance of recognizing their contributions to our shared history.

10.3.1 The Power of Collaboration

One of the key lessons we can learn from our ancient huntresses is the power of collaboration. Hunting was not an individual endeavor but a cooperative effort that required coordination and teamwork. Women played a crucial role in these group hunts, working alongside men to secure food for their communities. The success of these hunts relied on effective communication, trust, and the ability to work together towards a common goal. This collaborative spirit is a valuable lesson that we can apply to our modern lives, emphasizing the importance of teamwork and cooperation in achieving shared objectives.

10.3.2 Resilience and Adaptability

The lives of our ancient huntresses were marked by resilience and adaptability. They navigated diverse environments, honing their hunting skills to suit different terrains and prey. They faced challenges and overcame obstacles, demonstrating their ability to adapt to changing circumstances. This resilience and adaptability are qualities that we can draw inspiration from in our own lives. The recognition of women as skilled hunters highlights the strength and resourcefulness of our ancient ancestors, reminding us of the potential within ourselves to face adversity and thrive.

10.3.3 Breaking Gender Stereotypes

The existence of female hunters in prehistoric societies challenges deeply ingrained gender stereotypes. For too long, the assumption that men were the primary hunters and women were confined to domestic roles has shaped our understanding of the past. The discovery of female hunters disrupts these stereotypes and forces us to reevaluate our assumptions about gender roles. By recognizing the diversity of roles and capabilities within prehistoric societies, we can challenge and break down gender stereotypes in our own time. This lesson from our ancient huntresses encourages us to embrace gender equality and promote inclusivity in all aspects of life.

10.3.4 Environmental Stewardship

The hunting practices of our ancient ancestors were deeply connected to their environment. They understood the delicate balance of nature and the importance of sustainable hunting practices. Our ancient huntresses possessed a profound knowledge of the ecosystems they inhabited, allowing them to hunt in a way that ensured the long-term survival of their communities. This lesson in environmental stewardship is particularly relevant in our modern world, where the impact of human activities on the planet is increasingly evident. By learning from our ancient huntresses, we can strive to develop a more sustainable and harmonious relationship with the natural world.

10.3.5 Empowerment and Self-Expression

The recognition of female hunters in prehistoric societies empowers women today by providing historical evidence of their capabilities and contributions. It serves as a reminder that women have always played a vital role in shaping the course of human history. The stories of our ancient huntresses inspire us to embrace our own strengths and pursue our passions, regardless of societal expectations. Their existence challenges the notion that women are limited to certain roles and encourages us to celebrate and support the diverse talents and aspirations of all individuals.

10.3.6 A Call for Further Research

The revelations about female hunters in prehistoric societies highlight the importance of continued research and exploration. There are still many unanswered questions and gaps in our understanding of ancient gender roles. Further research, utilizing advancements in archaeological techniques and technologies, can provide us with a more comprehensive picture of our past. Collaborative and interdisciplinary approaches will be crucial in unraveling the complexities of prehistoric societies and shedding light on the lives of our ancient ancestors.

Conclusion

The recognition of female hunters in prehistoric societies challenges long-held assumptions and provides us with a more inclusive understanding of our shared history. The lessons we can learn from our ancient huntresses are numerous and far-reaching. Collaboration, resilience, breaking gender stereotypes, environmental stewardship, empowerment, and the call for further research are all valuable takeaways from this exploration. By embracing these lessons, we can strive for a more equitable and inclusive society, honoring the legacy of our ancient huntresses and shaping a better future for all.

10.4 Looking Ahead

As we conclude our exploration into the lives of ancient huntresses, it is crucial to reflect on the implications of recognizing their existence and the lessons we can learn from them. However, it is equally important to look ahead and consider the future of our understanding of prehistoric gender roles. The discoveries and research presented in this book have already challenged long-held assumptions and shed light on the egalitarian nature of our ancient ancestors. But there is still much more to uncover and explore.

10.4.1 Expanding the Scope of Research

The revelations about the existence of female hunters have opened up new avenues for research into prehistoric gender roles. As we move forward, it is essential to expand the scope of our investigations. While this book has primarily focused on the role of women as hunters, there are undoubtedly other aspects of gender roles that warrant further exploration.

For example, we have only scratched the surface when it comes to understanding the division of labor and responsibilities within prehistoric societies. By examining other aspects of daily life, such as tool-making, child-rearing, and social organization, we can gain a more comprehensive understanding of the dynamics between men and women in ancient communities.

10.4.2 Interdisciplinary Approaches

To further advance our understanding of prehistoric gender roles, it is crucial to embrace interdisciplinary approaches. Collaboration between archaeologists, anthropologists, paleontologists, geneticists, and other experts can provide a more holistic perspective on the lives of our ancient ancestors.

By combining different scientific methodologies and approaches, we can gain a deeper understanding of prehistoric societies. For example, genetic studies can provide insights into the movement and interactions of ancient populations, while archaeological excavations can uncover material evidence of gendered activities. By integrating these different sources of information, we can paint a more accurate picture of prehistoric gender roles.

10.4.3 Advancements in Technology

Advancements in archaeological techniques and technologies have the potential to revolutionize our understanding of prehistoric gender roles. As we continue to develop new methods for analyzing ancient artifacts, DNA, and isotopes, we can uncover previously hidden details about the lives of ancient huntresses.

For example, the use of high-resolution imaging techniques can reveal intricate details on ancient tools and weapons, providing insights into their construction and use. Isotopic analysis of skeletal remains can offer clues about diet and mobility patterns, helping us understand the roles individuals played within their communities. By staying at the forefront of technological advancements, we can continue to push the boundaries of our knowledge.

10.4.4 Collaborative Research

Collaboration among researchers from different regions and cultures is essential for a more inclusive understanding of prehistoric gender roles. By engaging with indigenous communities and incorporating their perspectives, we can gain valuable insights into the ways in which gender roles were shaped in different cultural contexts.

Furthermore, collaborative research can help address biases and assumptions that may exist within the field of archaeology. By working together, researchers can challenge each other's interpretations and ensure a more balanced and accurate representation of prehistoric gender roles.

10.4.5 Education and Awareness

Finally, it is crucial to disseminate the findings of our research to a wider audience. By educating the public about the existence of female hunters in prehistoric societies, we can challenge long-held stereotypes and promote a more inclusive understanding of gender roles.

This education should extend beyond academic circles and reach schools, museums, and community organizations. By raising awareness about the contributions of ancient huntresses, we can inspire future generations to question gender norms and challenge societal expectations.

In conclusion, the discoveries and research presented in this book have shattered the conventional portrayal of prehistoric gender roles. The existence of female hunters challenges long-held assumptions and highlights the egalitarian nature of our ancient ancestors. Looking ahead, it is essential to expand the scope of our research, embrace interdisciplinary approaches, utilize advancements in technology, foster collaborative research, and promote education and awareness. By doing so, we can continue to unravel the complexities of prehistoric gender roles and gain a more inclusive understanding of our shared human history.